D1372527

In praise of
Leadership on the Line . . .

"Thank you so much for your book. I shared it with our Guest Services Manager at our resort and she liked it so much she wanted her own copy, so I gave her mine. I want to order 8 more copies ... I just did our second program last week at our resort Divi Tiara, on Cayman Brac. They loved the books. Your book is a great tool for me!"

Ray Hobbs, Chief Operating Officer, Divi Resorts

"*Leadership on the Line* is the single best source of information for the development of strong service team leaders. I use it almost daily as a resource guide for the ongoing education of all service managers."

Chris Connor, General Manager, Peninsula Yacht Club, Cornelius, NC

"Got your book today ... and couldn't put it down! I love the format and how you used real life experiences. I wish I had read something like it years ago. This is fabulous!"

Wendy Hanavan, Meeting Planner, Olson Meeting Management, Raleigh, NC

"*Leadership on the Line* is the first great book I have read on how to become the best supervisor/leader you can be. This book is a must read for anyone entering the service business. You not only learn how to treat your employees and customers, you can learn how to better yourself and become a great team leader."

Allison Dettorre, Recreation Director, Northborough, MA

"*Leadership on the Line* fills a void that has existed in junior management training. It explains and reinforces the reasons why every service-based business exists. It does so in a broad enough manner that the material may be adapted to any size service business, or other industry for that matter."

Douglas C. Watters, President, Palm Canyon Resort, Borrego Spring, CA

"Full of no nonsense advice ... offers plenty of real-world examples. A copy of this book could make your work life a lot, lot easier."

Restaurant Hospitality

"*Leadership on the Line* [is] an incredible reference for employers or small business owners. I found so many answers to frustrating situations that need not interfere with everyday operations. Rehkopf highlights many solutions that could save failing programs and business relationships. I wish I had read this years ago."

Beth McAbee, Manager, The Square Onion Gourmet, Mt. Pleasant, SC

"*Leadership on the Line* . . . breaks down the concept of leadership to its most fundamental elements, then rebuilds it one brick at a time to ensure that the reader is on the 'same page' all the way. It is a primer, a timeless reference for all leaders . . . No manager [or] supervisor . . . should be without it."

Brian Moore, San Antonio, TX

"After 18 years in the industry you would think I know it all. Well your book proved me wrong. I really enjoyed your practical, no nonsense approach to team leadership and development."

Joel M. Stewart, CMP, Holiday Inn Downtown, Denver, CO

LEADERSHIP
ON THE LINE

A Guide for
Front Line Supervisors,
Business Owners, and Emerging Leaders

By
Ed Rehkopf

CLARITY PUBLICATIONS

Mooresville, North Carolina

ISBN 10: 0-9722193-1-5
ISBN 13: 978-0-9722193-1-0

To order, visit www.probizcom.com.

Printed and bound in the United States of America by

RJ Communications, New York

Acknowledgement

I wish to thank my wife, Clara, for her patient and tireless efforts to edit various versions of this book, as well as for providing its most appropriate title. Also, I am indebted to Charlie Nottingham, President of East West Partners Club Management; Lance Thompson, owner/operator of Henry's Bistro, both of Chapel Hill, North Carolina; and Robin Sandin, all for their careful readings of the manuscript and their many suggestions for improvement.

Table of Contents

Serving Your Customers

Serving Your Shareholders

Leaders Beware!

Practical Exercises

Summary

Related Articles

*This book is dedicated to all those
I have served with over the years – those
fine people who had to endure my
missteps along the way.*

"The longer I'm in business,
the more I realize it's all about leadership."

Tony Hyde, Executive Vice President
East West Partners Club Management

Service Breakdown
A Failure of Leadership

After thirty plus years in the hospitality business in both hotels and private clubs, I can state categorically that poor service comes from poor leadership. Show me an operation with poor, shoddy, inconsistent service, and I'll show you an organization with a failure of leadership. This observation flows from the understanding that leaders who recognize service problems in their organization will take corrective action. They will establish a plan of action, set priorities, lead employees to execute the plan, and follow through to completion.

Why, then, is poor service so often the rule rather than the exception? I have met many competent, hard-working, and professional general managers who voiced a clear and unequivocal service vision for their operations. They understood the need for well-defined standards, thorough training of employees, and constant reinforcement of service ideals within their organizations. Yet, they struggle to establish and maintain high standards of service. While we all recognize the many demands on our time, the challenge of employee turnover, the training burden in a detail-intensive business, time constraints, and ever-present budget pressures, these are not the root problem.

In examining this challenge that never seems to go away, I believe I have discovered the most significant source of the problem – the lack of well developed and consistent leadership skills among subordinate managers, those who direct the day-to-day activities of the operation's line employees. While the general manager may clearly understand and articulate the requirements of service, unless that "gospel" is communicated faithfully, consistently, and continuously to line employees by their immediate supervisors, there is a breakdown in the service message.

Throughout my career I have inherited or hired front line supervisors whose background, experience, or education should have prepared them for the challenges they would face daily in our business. While most had more than adequate technical skills to execute their responsibilities, they were often lacking in a critical aspect of leadership – how to direct and motivate employees to achieve high levels of quality and excellence.

While some front line supervisors demonstrated exceptional leadership skills, many did not. Often my biggest problems were created by supervisors who did not treat their employees properly, who did not communicate expectations, and who did not seem to understand or follow the most basic requirements of leading or managing people. These profound failings were crippling to the organization and required many hours of counseling, training, and, in some cases, terminations to remedy.

Over time I realized that any focus on training of line employees to smile and be friendly was a waste of time until I could be assured that my supervisors developed basic leadership skills. From that point on, I focused my efforts on training supervisors. Regardless of background or education, I wanted them to learn to be effective leaders, to paint and preach a vision of excellence for their staff, establish goals, communicate expectations, provide support and training to their employees, and solve the inevitable problems that arise when people work in a service context.

The training called for a clear vision for hospitality operations and guiding principles that would shape our efforts. I made it clear to supervisors that our employees were truly our most important resource, and they must be treated with dignity and respect.

Supervisors were told that their primary job was to provide direction, support, and training for their employees and that, based on their experience or education, I held them to a higher standard. I also provided detailed guidance on how to develop line employees and correctly counsel and discipline when necessary. Finally, I put a positive emphasis on communication and problem discovery. In time these concepts were formalized into a leaders' handbook which was issued to newly-hired supervisors.

How successful was I in achieving my ends? I would frankly admit that the results were mixed. While some supervisors responded positively, others seemed incapable or unwilling to grasp basic leadership principles. These, typically, after much invested time and effort, were encouraged to take their talents elsewhere. But on the whole, the effort yielded improved employee morale, lower turnover, better two-way communication, and a more upbeat team spirit among all staff. We still struggled with budget and time constraints on training, but we were far better off than we would have been without the effort.

Consistency and high levels of service will always be a challenge in business. Without competent and committed leaders at all levels, general managers will always be trying to "do it all." In time they will burn out or be forced to compromise their standards. In either case the result is service breakdown.

What follows evolved over the years and is presented here as a leadership guide. The concepts are broad enough to apply anywhere in any industry attempting to deliver high quality service and to develop employees to their fullest potential.

Ed Rehkopf

Service-based Leadership

Success in Business

The purpose of any business is to provide a product or service for its customers, make a profit for its owners or shareholders, and maintain itself as a "going concern," that is, a business that intends on staying in business. In today's highly competitive marketplace, where many companies are vying to provide similar products and services, often the only distinction between enterprises is the level and quality of service provided.

Realizing this, it would not be an overstatement to say that the nature of business is SERVICE. As a supervisor all your efforts and those of your employees are directed toward providing the highest possible level of service to customers. To do this you must anticipate their needs and desires, set standards of excellence that challenge employees, train continually, and constantly examine and improve the details of your operation.

The success of your efforts and the excellence of your operation are ultimately measured ONLY by customer satisfaction. And it is only through the dedicated efforts of your willing workers that you can consistently achieve customer satisfaction.

Success in business is simple in concept, but difficult in execution. In simplest terms, successful businesses give their customers what they want, at a price they think is fair, with the expected level of service. The formula for success can be expressed as:

Right Product + Right Price + Right Service

Given that, in most companies, senior managers determine product and pricing, the supervisor's arena of influence is service and service delivery. While this is only one-third of the overall equation for success, it is the most difficult component, and the challenge comes ultimately from one source – PEOPLE.

People are complex, carry lots of personal baggage, are often poor communicators, and are sometimes defensive, quick to lash out and place blame. Often they have agendas hidden even to themselves; they suffer various insecurities and lack clear aims. These people are your customers, your employees, and the owners or shareholders of your company.

The Leader's Role

As a supervisor your role is to keep all of these people relatively happy and satisfied, and in the case of employees, to keep them focused on the task at hand. The difficulty is that the needs and desires of these constituencies are often in direct competition. Employees want realistic wages and satisfying work. Customers want value and service. Shareholders want to be associated with a high quality enterprise and to maximize the return on their investment. The job of the supervisor is to balance these competing needs. If one gets out of balance, the other two suffer.

"Balancing the needs of all constituencies requires exceptional leadership skill."

For example, employees are unhappy with poor working conditions and request a new break area. Shareholders don't want to bear the expense. Poor employee morale affects the customers who sense hostility and a less-than-helpful attitude. Customers pick up on the bad vibes and take their business elsewhere. The decrease in sales reduces profit and ultimately the shareholders' return on investment. Everyone is unhappy and blames the leader.

Not only must you be an outstanding leader, capable of maintaining a positive attitude in the face of daily challenges, but you must also remain focused on goals, lead by inspiration and example, and hold employees accountable for results. Further, you must be able to maintain this effort and pace over the long haul. Clearly, this requires men and women of uncommon talent, dedication, drive, and temperament.

Leadership

What is Leadership?

Many books have been written to define what constitutes leadership, the role of the leader, the essential traits of leadership, and the habits of successful leaders. Without adding anything new to this body of work, I simply list the following abbreviated definitions from The Random House College Dictionary:

> To lead: go before or with to show the way; guide in direction, course, action, opinion; influence; command or direct an organization; go at the head of or in advance of.

> Leader: a person who leads, a guiding or directing head of an organization.

Leadership: the position or function of a leader; the ability to lead; an act or instance of leading.

Given that each of these definitions ultimately involves guiding, influencing, and directing people, I posit the following working definition for this handbook:

Leadership is the sum of those individual traits, skills, and abilities that allow one person to commit and direct the efforts of others toward the accomplishment of a particular objective.

Central to this definition is the understanding that exercising leadership involves building and sustaining relationships between leader and followers. Without this bond or connection, there are no willing followers and, therefore, no true leader. Given that no leader operates in a vacuum, it also requires the leader to establish relationships with other relevant constituencies.

A Few Observations on Leadership

Every group enterprise demands a leader. The absence of leadership in a group creates a vacuum that someone will rise to fill. If a leader is not appointed, then one will naturally emerge. I've read that when a group of chickens loses its rooster, a hen will stop laying eggs and take on the dominant role, providing protection and leadership to the flock. In a business setting where the appointed manager fails to provide leadership, one of the workers will rise to become the *de facto* or shadow leader, sometimes at odds with the purposes of management.

Because the quality of leadership is always examined in hindsight when success has been won, we look to the leader with reverence and awe. Often his or her life and accomplishments take on mythical proportions. Thus leadership has become an almost sacred word, wrapped in an aura of mysterious gift and ability. In this light, leadership is always good since it is always applied to the successful. A failed leader is no leader at all. But this is always the historical judgment. For those attempting to lead at this moment, the jury is still out.

Just as a highly competitive basketball game cannot be won without the talent, commitment, and the effort of all players, so a leader facing a challenge or working toward a particular goal needs the willing commitment of all employees. Without this commitment, the leader is handicapped from the outset and will find success neither complete nor easy to come by.

As there are many types of leaders – political, intellectual, military, industrial, business, financial, athletic, and so on for any conceivable endeavor and profession – the skills and abilities that might make a person successful in one arena do not necessarily guarantee success in another.

Many people hold positions of authority by virtue of ownership, heredity, education, oratorical skill, appointment, election, circumstances, or even bluff, but the exercise of authority doesn't necessarily make them leaders. The position of President, CEO, General, Doctor, or Professor may command respect, deference, even fear, but they do not necessarily have the willing commitment and loyalty of their followers unless this has been earned by the exercise of leadership.

There are various styles of leadership – the most common ones being autocratic, collegial, nurturing, and moral/ethical. There are successful models of each style. General George Patton was an autocratic leader; Mahatma Gandhi was a moral/ethical leader. Some leaders such as Abraham Lincoln and Winston Churchill used a mix of styles.

Leadership Principles

Principles common to all successful leaders regardless of their outward presentation have been listed in many different forms and contexts, but are remarkably similar in their essence. A representative list of leadership principles includes:

◆ Be professionally and technically proficient.
◆ Respect and show concern for those you lead.
◆ Set the example.
◆ Know your capabilities and seek self-improvement.
◆ Understand your mission.
◆ Communicate your expectations.
◆ Instill motivation and morale in those you lead.
◆ Build teamwork.
◆ Make sound and timely decisions.
◆ Develop your subordinates.
◆ Ensure tasks are understood, properly supervised, and accomplished.
◆ Be responsible for your actions.

While different leadership styles are suited to different personalities and situations, the underlying leadership principles seldom vary and are essential to any successful leader. To the extent that you possess and practice these principles, you will be successful. To the extent that you are lacking in these principles, you will be handicapped, or will fail outright, in your endeavors.

Leadership Traits

By conscientiously and consistently applying the foregoing principles, leaders develop character traits that become the foundation for all the skills and techniques employed to achieve success. These traits will include:

◆ The will to make things happen.

◆ Willingness to take and stand by an unpopular view.

◆ The ability to pace oneself and go the distance.

◆ Loyalty to the company, superiors, and employees.

◆ Willingness to make decisions based upon the best available information and analysis.

◆ Dependability and consistency.

◆ Integrity and truthfulness.

◆ Fairness.

◆ Good judgment.

◆ Willingness to share praise and shoulder blame.

◆ Professional decorum, understanding the correct time and place for everything.

◆ Enthusiasm.

Application of Leadership Skills

Leadership is situational. Different situations and people require the application of different sets of skills and techniques. What works for the General may not work for the Politician. The art of leadership, then, is in the ability to size up a given situation and understand how best to address it.

While some leaders have an innate sense of what to do, most learn through experience. Unfortunately for first-time supervisors, such experience is in short supply. Some of you are lucky enough to have been mentored by a respected senior leader or you have worked for someone who taught leadership by example. But whatever your experience, much of your success or failure will come from your attitudes about the job and the people you lead.

In extreme cases, new supervisors believe that it is only through their efforts that progress is made, that employees can't be trusted, that goals can only be achieved by driving people hard, and that discipline is the only way to keep staff in line. Quite naturally, these attitudes create an environment where employees are fearful. Such fear-based management is damaging to your service team and, ultimately, to the company. Consider the case of Michael, an eager first-time supervisor.

Michael was a bright and ambitious recent graduate of a respected university. He was hired based upon his enthusiasm, energy, and obvious intelligence. The company expected great things of him.

Sure enough, there were immediate results. He analyzed his department's operation and identified areas for improvement. He presented his superiors with a detailed action plan and a timeline for accomplishment. As the months passed, he met each deadline and his department's numbers were showing a definite positive trend. Senior management could not have been more pleased. Michael was quickly establishing himself as a rising star in the company.

However, seven months after Michael started, his assistant manager, Willard, a longstanding and trusted employee, abruptly resigned. In his exit interview with Human Resources, Willard was bitter in his denunciation of Michael and of the company for hiring him and failing to properly supervise him.

It seems that Michael's meteoric success had been built upon a hard-nosed, bullying management style. He frequently flew into tirades if his employees did not perform to his expectations, yet he was a poor communicator, rarely meeting with his staff to explain his goals or desires. Further, Willard said he often berated his employees in front of others.

According to Willard, departmental morale had never been lower. When Willard tried to talk to Michael about mounting staff resentment, Michael threatened him, saying that Willard was conspiring to undermine his authority. The last straw occurred when Michael complained to line employees about his assistant's performance.

Unfortunately, Willard could not be dissuaded from retiring, but in the ensuing investigation his allegations were borne out. In reviewing departmental records, investigators found a higher incidence of absenteeism, much departmental rework masked by unauthorized overtime, and a deep and pervasive anger on the part of the staff.

As a result of the investigation, Michael was reassigned to another division. His boss was disciplined for lax supervision, and the company worked hard to regain the trust of its employees. While the situation eventually returned to normal, the affair disrupted the smooth operation of the company for over two years.

Fear-based Management

Fear-based management is rooted in the insecurities of the supervisor. While most people have insecurities, in this instance, the immature, inexperienced, and untrusting attitude of the supervisor dominates the workplace. Some symptoms of fear-based management are:

◆ Employees covering their backsides.
◆ Unwillingness to take a risk.
◆ Lack of initiative and acceptance of the status quo.
◆ Employees afraid to express opinions or answer questions.
◆ Lack of trust.
◆ Defensiveness and blame placing.
◆ Lack of communication or only top-down communication.
◆ Poor motivation and morale.
◆ Lack of cheerfulness, friendliness, and smiles.

Fear-based management impedes organizational teamwork and effectiveness but can be overcome by a leader with an open, trusting attitude and a willingness to grow both as a person and a leader. Because of its detrimental impact on employees, customers, and the bottom line, fear-based management should not be tolerated in any company.

Service-based Leadership

At the other end of the spectrum is the ideal of service-based leadership. With this approach, the attitude and primary motivation of the leader is service to others – to customers, to employees, to shareholders. This approach to leadership naturally creates relationships – the deep and abiding bonds that sustain the efforts of the company. This outward focus of the leader sets up a dynamic where:

- Employees are continually recognized.
- There is an open flow of ideas, opinions, and information.
- Initiative and risk are highly regarded.
- Problem discovery and solution is a focus while placing blame is unimportant.
- Every employee feels energized and part of the team and is valued for his or her contribution.
- Prestige is derived from performance and contribution, not title or position.
- Customers are treated well because employees are treated well.
- The energy and initiative of all employees is focused on the common effort.

With service-based leadership, you will find that good customer service to both internal and external customers is effortless. Less energy is expended in processing complaints, grievances, and conflicts. Work is more fun and everyone's job is easier.

While it may be difficult for a new supervisor to accept these facts without the proof of experience, keep an open mind. Later in this book, you will be given some exercises that, when applied, will demonstrate the effectiveness of a service-based approach to leadership.

Building Strong Relationships

Maggie was a retired schoolteacher starting a second career. She applied for a sales associate position with a well-known hotel and conference center. While she had no sales experience, her maturity, calm demeanor, and articulate style impressed the Director of Sales.

The position of sales associate is challenging. In addition to selling the facility and its services to the local community and industry, it is important to have a good working relationship with the hotel's operating departments. Ultimately, they are the ones who must execute the promises of the sales staff.

In short order, Maggie proved adept at winning new business for the hotel. She had a knack for meeting new people and establishing a sense of trust. Much of it came from her genuine, down-to-earth nature. She was short on hype and easy promises, but long on establishing meaningful relationships built upon commitment, confidence, and trust. Her clients knew that she was true to her word.

But as strong as she was in finding new business, she was even stronger at building those key relationships with hotel department heads and line employees enabling her to ensure that promises were kept and expectations met. Inevitably things would fall through the cracks and some meeting room was not set up properly for one of her clients. Maggie, because she always double-checked arrangements, would find the problem and seek help to correct it. Because she had taken the time to develop good working relations with the housekeeping, maintenance, and banquet staffs, she never had problems finding someone willing to help. As one porter said of her, "She always asks so nicely, there is no way to say no."

Maggie was an outstanding success as a sales associate. In two years she increased her hotel bookings by 18.3%, and more importantly, trend lines promised even more future business from her many satisfied clients. Not surprisingly, when the Director of Sales was transferred to another property out of state, Maggie was asked by her General Manager to take over the position.

Your success in balancing the needs of those you serve lies in ensuring that you build strong relationships with individuals. How do you do this? Begin by:

◆ Treating everyone you meet with courtesy, respect, and good cheer.

◆ Focusing on each person you deal with as if he or she were the most important person in the world.

◆ Taking the time to get to know people; sharing your time and attention with them.

◆ Learning about other people's jobs and the challenges and difficulties they face.

◆ Keeping promises and following through on commitments.

◆ Being principled, showing fairness, and demonstrating integrity.

◆ Recognizing the ultimate value of people in all you do.

Relationships depend upon how you view yourself in relation to others. If you see yourself as separate and apart from your constituencies, if you view others as the means to your end, if your vision and goals lack a broader purpose than your own needs and ambitions, establishing meaningful relationships will be impossible. On the other hand, when you see yourself as part of a team with a shared mission, then a sense of service will be an intrinsic part of your service team relationships.

The difference is your attitude, your motives, and your approach to dealing with others. Since all of these things are within your power to change, establishing a service-based approach to leadership by building strong relationships is totally up to you.

Summary

Success in business comes from delivering the right product at the right price with the expected level of service.

Often the only distinction between competitors is the level and quality of service provided.

Your role in the company is to deliver service.

These responsibilities cannot be adequately met without the committed involvement of your employees.

Leadership is the sum of those individual traits, skills, and abilities that allow one person to commit and direct the efforts of others toward the accomplishment of a particular objective.

There are a number of styles of leadership, but all are founded on certain leadership principles.

A common mistake for new supervisors is to manage by fear. Fear-based management is detrimental to a company's operation.

With service-based leadership, the attitude of the leader is one of service to employees, customers, and shareholders.

Building strong relationships is the key to demonstrating a service-based approach to leadership.

Becoming a Service-based Leader

By conscientiously following and practicing the principles of leadership, by working to develop the traits of service-based leadership, you can become an effective leader in any situation. As a first-time leader in a service industry, your focus should be on those employees who make up your service team.

Leading Your Service Team

Line employees are the most important staff a company has because they interface directly with customers. Their daily performance in meeting customers' needs establishes and maintains a company's good name and reputation. Clearly their performance is critical to a company's success.

Shoddy, surly, disorganized, and inconsistent service are clear signs of a lack of leadership. Employees are not to blame; rather it is management that must be held accountable. Conversely, high standards of service flow naturally from effective leaders. Your service team's performance is a direct result of your leadership. This leadership must include taking personal responsibility, possessing the will to lead, owning your failures, effectively utilizing your resources, and knowing your limits.

The Freedom of Taking Personal Responsibility

Personal freedom is often thought of as the absence of responsibility. In this respect, no one is free. Everyone is responsible for and to someone else. There is, however, a freedom that comes from accepting personal responsibility for oneself and one's sphere of influence.

When you blame no one else for the challenges you face, when you realize that where you stand today is the result of all your past decisions and indecision, you look to the true source of any difficulties. It is never the undefined "they." It is always the ever present "I."

Realizing this is the true source of your freedom. Instead of being buffeted to and fro by uncontrollable forces, you accept the power of your own authority. For good or ill, you are the one in charge of your life.

For the supervisor, this means that, as you seek opportunity, you also take responsibility for all aspects of your duties. Size up those around you: your superiors, peers, and employees. If they demonstrate responsibility, learn to depend upon them. If they don't, find ways to compensate for their inadequacies. In the case of your employees, take action as necessary.

In the end, you are the only one responsible for your success or failure. If something goes wrong, there is always more you could have done. In the case of the truly unexpected event, it's not so much what went wrong as how you respond to it. Instead of blaming circumstances or others, take responsibility to make things right. By accepting this degree of personal responsibility, you free yourself from the unpredictability of life and those around you.

The Will to Lead

Taking personal responsibility equips you to assume a leadership role. But the will to lead is a far cry from being willing to lead. A good number of people are willing to accept positions of leadership. But accepting and exercising leadership are two very different matters.

Having the will to lead implies a commitment to face whatever challenges may present themselves. Simply put, it's the will to make things happen. Consider this example.

Bob was the front desk manager of an older hotel. Hospitality was his profession, but running was his passion. Each day at lunchtime, regardless of the weather, he took a five-mile run. After running he used the employee locker room to shower and change before returning to work.

The poor sanitation and maintenance of the locker rooms disgusted Bob, but for a long time he said nothing. Finally, he had enough and announced at a staff meeting that the employees deserved better and that he was going to petition the General Manager to clean and fix up the locker rooms.

One of the other supervisors commented that it would be a waste of time and that they would quickly return to their former condition. He said that the employees didn't care and wouldn't keep them up. Bob responded that it didn't matter whether the employees cared or not – he did!

Over the next few weeks with the General Manager's blessing, Bob organized the maintenance and housekeeping staffs to scrape and repaint walls, strip and refinish the floor, replace broken and unserviceable lockers, and improve the lighting. Then he got the General Manager to assign different departments the rotating duty of keeping the locker rooms clean. Finally, he checked them daily for several months to ensure that they were being properly maintained.

The end result was improved employee morale and a changed attitude about their locker rooms. Employees did care – they just needed someone to lead the way and to overcome the erroneous notion that they didn't. They needed Bob's "will to make things happen."

Owning Your Failures

When you or those you lead fail in any way, don't make excuses. While there may be mitigating circumstances, you must take responsibility for the failure. Whether you didn't plan or train well enough, didn't devote the proper time or resources to the matter, didn't establish priorities, or underestimated the situation, the bottom line is that you failed. But failure can become your most valuable learning tool!

Rather than casting about for others to blame, carefully analyze what led to the failure and see what you might have done differently to achieve a positive outcome. This approach accomplishes two very important things:

◆ You establish your personal responsibility and authority, and

◆ You analyze and learn from your mistakes.

Do not be afraid to make mistakes. No one is error free, and those claiming to be take few risks. Leadership is distinguished by leading, not by hanging back in the pack. When you step forward to lead, you risk the chance of highly visible missteps. Remember that experience and "trial and error" can be life's most powerful instructors.

Often the greatest lessons are learned from mistakes. Winning breeds a sense of supremacy and complacency; whereas losing encourages critical review. Keep this in mind as you blunder along the way. While I've had some success in my career, I can honestly say that my most memorable lessons came from mistakes and failure.

Years ago in my first hotel, I took a proprietary interest in all aspects of the operation to the point of guarding its assets as if they were my own. While caring about one's operation is laudable, in one case I clearly lost sight of the larger picture.

One busy football weekend I was monitoring activity near the front entrance. A gentleman passed me carrying one of our beer glasses. I approached him and politely asked him if I could return the glass to the bar for him. One thing led to another until we had a full-blown confrontation over a 79-cent glass.

In hindsight this upsetting incident was unnecessary. Glassware loss from breakage and pilferage is part of the cost of doing business. The time and emotional aggravation related to this incident were not worth the insignificant cost of the glass. Add to this the complete alienation of a customer and all the people to whom he related his "horror" story.

Since that time I have come to understand that there are a number of "costs" in business that should be monitored and controlled in a systematic way, not by personal confrontation. This lesson learned was a small one, but one I shall never forget.

Effectively Using Your Limited Resources

There is far more to do every day than you can possibly accomplish. Where you apply your time and energy as a supervisor is of critical importance to your team's efforts and success. Avoid frittering away your personal resources on marginal activities. Focus on the important things that will make a difference in your team's performance.

To do this you should make a list of the key items on which to focus and have a long-term plan of improvement for your operation, as well as a list of needed projects to accomplish. Despite the daily distractions and crises that inevitably come up, keep your focus on those key items. When things slow down or windows of time open up, refocus yourself and your team on those important goals.

It's also helpful to get away from your operations, even for just a day. Being away from the day-to-day problems will give a broader perspective on the issues you face and will help you recognize where to apply yourself.

Recognizing the Limits of Your Influence

Being an effective supervisor requires that you understand the parameters of your authority and the extent of your sphere of influence. For instance, what should you do when you report to a superior who lacks essential leadership skills?

Remember the freedom of taking personal responsibility. You cannot control your boss' skill or lack of it, but instead of getting upset, focus on what you can control. Do everything in your power to be the best leader you can be. Try to insulate your team from the worst effects of the situation. Do not disparage your boss in front of your employees. They will size up the situation quickly enough and will respect you even more for not trying to make him look bad.

Possibly your efforts will have a positive effect on your boss. If your area of the operation is performing well because of your leadership, it may cause him to take notice. Maybe your boss will become curious enough to ask about the secrets of your success. In any case, focus on your own efforts. If the situation should become untenable, remember that you retain ultimate control over your future and can make the appropriate decision at any time.

Understanding the limits of your influence also entails the recognition that you have more impact and control over your employees than you do over your other constituencies. Your customers are removed from your direct influence since they are served by your employees. For the most part your influence on customers is secondhand.

Farthest removed from your influence are your company's shareholders. Unless as owners they take a direct role in your company, they are often absent from the operation. Their role and status with the company is still of major importance, but their interests are served at a distance.

So as you work to accomplish your company's goals, concentrate on those nearest at hand and those over whom you have the greatest influence – the employees on your service team. If they do their jobs with enthusiasm and a sense of service, the needs of your other constituencies will also be met.

Problems as Opportunities to Lead

Every problem is a gift in disguise. It brings to light something that can be done to make the organization function more efficiently. Having a negative attitude toward problems blinds you to solutions.

Problems should be solved at the lowest possible level. Senior leaders are responsible for charting the course of the company and planning for the future. The more time they spend dealing with day-to-day operating problems, the less able they are to fulfill those roles.

Be Proactive in Finding Problems

Every organization has problems, but some managers try to hide them. A sure sign that there are problems is that no one ever talks about them. Everything seems to go too smoothly; no one wants to rock the boat or else they are in deep denial. It is a simple task to ask questions, to dig a little wherever you go. Inevitably problems turn up. Often those most familiar with and vocal about problems are the employees who deal with them every day.

A significant step in solving problems is to place a major and positive emphasis on problem discovery. It's the first step in problem solution. As a leader, your performance is not measured by how few problems you have, rather by how many are being actively addressed. Senior leaders expect to hear about problems from you, not from your employees or customers.

Every Problem Has a Solution

There may not be an ideal solution, but there will be a solution. Many problems are complex and involve other areas of the company. Setting priorities and being willing to work as a team play large parts in solving interrelated problems.

You may also need to break large problems down into their component parts. This often points the way to a solution. The many small steps taken to correct a problem frequently involve compromises. Do not be discouraged if no perfect solution exists; find one that solves the greatest part of the problem, or is the easiest to implement, or gives the biggest bang for the buck.

Brainstorming with other leaders or with employees can provide insights into solving large and complex problems. Do not hesitate to use your employees' knowledge of the operation to help find solutions.

Finally, solutions cannot be implemented in a vacuum. Examine how proposed solutions might affect other parts of the company and coordinate implementation accordingly.

Design System Solutions

Quick fixes usually do not address the underlying causes of problems. By examining, improving, and documenting the process, you can establish underlying systems that will routinely handle situations. When the bulk of situations in a business are handled routinely, more time is available for customer service and paying attention to details.

Attempt to follow the 90-10 rule. If you have established routine system procedures for your operation, you are able to devote 90% of your efforts to 10% of the operation – the most critical details. Look at how one recurring problem was solved with the development of an efficient system.

Joanne was the beverage manager in a high-end country club. One of her responsibilities was the beverage cart service provided on the golf course. The challenge presented by this service was a lack of inventory control over readily consumable and easily pilfered snack items. Predictably, the club had ongoing problems. After continually suspecting employees and worrying about unidentified losses, Joanne designed a system of checks and balances.

The beverage cart attendant was required to draw inventory from the golf course snack bar. The snack bar attendant completed the inventory issue sheet and noted all issues as well as turn-ins at the end of the day. The beverage cart attendant kept track of sales on an inventory sold sheet. Both forms were turned in to Joanne daily, giving her an easy way to compare both sales and inventory consumption.

The system was not foolproof, was subject to daily counting errors, and could be overcome by collusion among employees. But for the most part, it worked well and gave Joanne a routine tool to monitor beverage cart sales. Systems don't have to be complex or highly sophisticated; they just have to work.

Adding Value to Your Company

Leadership also means being someone who consistently adds value to his or her company. There are a number of ways to accomplish this end; start by rejecting the status quo, managing your boss, and taking initiative.

Reject the Status Quo

When confronted with some policy or procedure that does not make sense or seems overly burdensome, ask if there is not a better way. Often when you begin to ask questions as to why things are done a certain way, the response will be "I don't know; we've always done it that way." This is a sure sign that everyone is sleepwalking through the process.

Finding the organizational dysfunction is the easy part; the challenge comes in examining all aspects of the process to come up with a better way – a way that makes sense from all perspectives. Don't just go to your boss complaining about how stupid a procedure is, take her a well-thought out plan to streamline or transform the system.

Several years ago I went to work for a large governmental agency. During my in-processing, I was required to visit a half dozen offices and fill out at least a dozen forms, most requiring the same basic information.

Not only did I waste a lot of time traveling from one location to another, but this introduction to my new employer gave me little cause for confidence. While trying to bear the ordeal with patience and equanimity, I realized that this was the experience of all new employees to the organization – certainly not a good first impression.

Shortly after this experience, I proposed that the entire process be set up in one office. By using an off-the-shelf computer database, a new employee could sit down at a computer terminal and enter all the information at one time. The program could print out all the various forms necessary for in-processing. The employee could then sign the various forms, which would be sent to the requiring agencies. A further benefit of a computer-generated process was that all the forms would be legible and all the information consistent.

While large bureaucracies are among the most difficult to change, the exercise of developing alternatives enhanced my leadership skills and prepared me for challenges where those skills could effect change. Never complain – always occupy yourself with solutions.

Manage Your Boss

Randy was the long-standing maintenance supervisor in a hotel that I was hired to manage. My first impressions of him were not good. The property was poorly maintained and he always had excuses for the many problems of the hotel.

As I began to dig deeper and deeper into the challenges of the hotel, Randy took to stopping by my office each morning. While I was anxious to learn as much as I could from him, each morning became a litany of complaints, usually that he did not have the necessary tools, staff, or time to take care of all the things for which his department was responsible. Frequently, he disparaged his employees and their lack of necessary skills. Further, I had the distinct sense that Randy was looking to me for solutions to his problems, both real and imagined.

After repeated attempts to prod Randy into positive action, I had a serious heart-to-heart with him. In particular I told him that if I had to make all his decisions and solve his problems, I clearly didn't need him. Unexpectedly he resigned on the spot. While surprised by his sudden action, I was relieved to see him go. On an interim basis, I appointed John, his assistant, to run the department.

From the day he took over, John made a huge difference. He reorganized the department, held weekly meetings with his staff, presented me with requests for tools and equipment supported by detailed justification and cost/benefit analyses, established a new work order system, met with department heads to foster improved communications, designed a guest room preventive maintenance system, and provided me with weekly and monthly reports of his actions and progress.

Like Randy, John also stopped by my office each day for a few minutes. But he never complained; he only kept me informed of what he was working on. Sometimes he sought my permission to pursue a particular course of action or sought confirmation of his plans. With each passing day I grew less and less concerned about maintenance. Confidence in John and the job he was doing allowed me to turn my attention to other pressing matters.

Two months later I suspended the search for a new maintenance chief – I had already found my leader in John!

As a leader, you are responsible for influencing your boss' perceptions of your work and performance. Keep your boss informed of the problems you're working on. Periodic summary reports showing operational trends, improved performance, and greater efficiencies keep her better informed and influence perceptions of your performance.

Keep in mind that she has large responsibilities, is often very busy, yet still has the need to know what is going on in the organization. Assuring your boss that you are aware of and actively working on problems sets her mind at ease. In this regard you are seen as someone who helps make your boss' job easier.

Don't be afraid to seek guidance from your boss. One of her responsibilities is to provide direction to your efforts. Most bosses are open to questions and concerns, so long as you do not dominate their time or use them as a crutch in your own decision-making.

If you go to your boss with a problem, make sure you have a recommended solution. This allows her to agree with your thinking and problem-solving approach without being expected to do your job for you.

Also, the members of your service team will see how managing your boss enhances the team's stature in the eyes of higher management. Nothing is better for staff morale than knowing that your own supervisor is highly regarded by her superiors.

Let Service Begin with You!

In attempting to affect positive change in your company, do not wait for others to do their part. Whether your boss or your peers believe in or apply the principles of service-based leadership, make your contribution by taking the initiative. In time, your example will have an unmistakable impact on all around you.

To the extent that your leadership efforts are based upon service to others rather than your personal ambitions, your success will be magnified. Employees will more willingly dedicate themselves to any endeavor when part of a team effort and when they feel that their interests are also being served.

Summary

The success of your service team depends on you.

To ensure success, take personal responsibility, cultivate a will to lead, recognize and own your failures, effectively utilize your resources, and recognize your limits.

Problems provide opportunities to lead if you actively look for them, work with your team to find solutions, and design system-solutions to deal with "routine" problems.

Add value to your company by rejecting the status quo, by "managing your boss," and by taking initiative.

Serving Your Employees

A supervisor's primary constituency is staff. They are the people over whom the leader has the most influence and control. They are the people who provide service to your customers.

In some companies, employees are treated merely as a means to an end – the end of making as much money as possible for the company. Little concern is shown for the employees' work environment, very little time is devoted to training, and employees must often make do under difficult circumstances without the support of their superiors. This should not be the way you treat those who are routinely claimed to be a company's "most important resource."

Your ultimate concern is satisfying the customer, and how your employees are treated has an immediate and direct bearing on how customers are treated. Employees who feel good about themselves, whose welfare and problems are attended to in a supportive way, who are provided with the right tools and training to do their jobs, will continually and enthusiastically communicate their satisfaction to customers in countless small ways.

As a leader, therefore, it is in your best interest to be as supportive of employees as possible. They are the people without whom you could not do your job. If they are unhappy and dissatisfied, they will feel no loyalty to you or the company. You will constantly be dealing with customer complaints about staff and service, continually enduring employee turnover with its attendant training burden, and forever suffering from the turmoil created by unhappy people.

Principles of Employee Relations

By creating and sustaining a work environment that promotes a happy and satisfied staff, you ensure a positive customer experience. To stress the importance of employees, you should fully embrace the following principles:

◆ Treat employees with dignity and respect. Do not permit the workplace to become a hostile environment for any employee.

◆ Conduct your employee relations in an honest and straightforward way. Any necessary criticism or counseling must be conducted in private in a constructive manner with the intention of educating rather than blaming.

◆ Stress to your staff that every employee contributes to the overall success of the company. The only difference among employees is their level of authority and responsibility. Every employee is important!

◆ Realize that when employees fail, it is often a failure of management to properly train or communicate performance expectations. You can only expect employees to do something properly if you have properly shown them how to do it.

◆ Communicate to your employees what goals you have for them. Employees have a need and the right to know how their performance is contributing to the achievement of those goals. Provide ongoing feedback.

◆ Make practical efforts to keep employees informed on matters concerning policy, procedures, long-range plans, projects, work conditions, compensation, and benefits. Be available at reasonable times to answer questions and hear employee concerns.

◆ Recognize employees for their successes. You have the authority to correct, so you must also accept the responsibility to praise and reward.

◆ Strive to make the workplace interesting, challenging, and rewarding. When appropriate, involve employees in the decision-making process. The ideas and energy of employees will be a major contributor to your success.

◆ Challenge employees to do everything possible within good taste and reason to make the workplace more enjoyable.

Directing Employees

Directing employees is one of the hardest and most time-consuming things a leader does, particularly in a labor-intensive business. It is also the most important. Unless you work totally alone and have no contact with others, in which case you wouldn't be a leader, you must develop the leadership skills to work with and direct others.

A number of years ago I hired a brilliant young chef to run the food service of a club I managed. The members had been clamoring for high-quality, innovative food, so when the opportunity presented itself, I brought Tony on board.

True to expectations Tony produced awesome food. The members were blown away and the rave reviews poured in. While I was thrilled with his food, it wasn't long before I sensed that all was not right in the kitchen.

The Dining Room Manager came to me several times to tell me that Tony repeatedly blew up at the wait staff. It finally got so bad that waiters were afraid to go into the kitchen. There was even a case of his blowing up at a housekeeper who was getting her employee meal. I also noticed that the kitchen seemed to be a revolving door for cooks and dishwashers.

I finally called one of the recently resigned cooks to find out what was going on. He said that Tony never trained his kitchen staff and rarely communicated his goals or requirements. He also said Tony was a hard worker, but was often moody and didn't seem to trust his employees. As a result, Tony felt he had to be in the kitchen at all hours. His temper became shorter and shorter as he understandably began to burn out. While I repeatedly encouraged him to take time off and to soften his approach to his employees, he was clearly unreceptive to counsel.

Less than six months after he was hired, Tony suddenly quit. The job had taken a tremendous toll on him physically and emotionally. While Tony's cooking was spectacular, his leadership and interpersonal skills were sadly lacking. He had alienated other departments and his own staff was happy to see him go.

In many ways Tony's story was a tragedy. He was incredibly talented, yet had a serious overarching flaw. He could not direct or even get along with others. Repeated counseling could not help him see the light. I could only hope that someday his disappointments would cause him to examine this failing.

People are complex and unique. They have their own ideas, experiences, and problems. As a leader you have to get them to accept the goals, standards, procedures, and culture of the company. If you do nothing else well as a leader, you must manage people well. The following ideas will help you to direct your employees:

◆ Telling an employee to do something is only the first and smallest part of the job. Constantly remind your employees of the important things. What is seen as important to you becomes important to them. Never give the excuse that you told an employee to do something – check to ensure that it was done and done right. Check and double-check.

◆ When you tell employees to do something, set a deadline or give priorities, so they have some sense of how important or urgent the matter is. If you have a deadline or require a response, say so.

◆ Get out and move about. If you are in your office all day, you are not doing your job. You should be "out and about" 60-70% of your time – checking and double-checking. Being actively involved in your operation sends a powerful message to employees. It says you care about what is going on.

◆ Explain the "big picture" to your employees. They need to understand how their efforts contribute to the larger goals of the company.

◆ Never raise your voice or lose control when directing employees.

◆ You may correct employees' work or behavior, but never be demeaning or criticize them personally. Employees' self esteem is essential to their success and yours.

◆ Never correct employees before you have determined all the facts. Don't allow your biases and assumptions to blind you to other perspectives. Consult with other leaders to gain fresh perspectives on particularly difficult situations.

◆ Rules and standards should be spelled out in detail, talked about often, and enforced. If you don't enforce them, you might as well not have them. Nobody likes to play the bad guy, but it's preferable to being wishy-washy. If your employees know where you stand and you're consistent, there is no confusion.

While you will undoubtedly have some problem employees whose dedication, skills, attitude, or enthusiasm are lacking, these must be treated as the exception. If you have many such employees, it may be a reflection of your leadership.

Training Employees

Employee Development

As a group of people committed to common goals, you can only achieve your team's greatest potential by taking advantage of the talent, initiative, and ingenuity of each and every one of your employees. To the extent that any individual is not valued, trained, and motivated, your enterprise suffers.

It is the responsibility of leaders at all levels of the company to ensure that employees are developed to their fullest potential and that they are trained in all aspects of their jobs. Because most businesses are large and complex, involving hundreds of details, there is much for employees to know.

From the company's perspective, the desired outcome of the hiring process is to hire, train, and retain quality people who will make a positive contribution to the success of the enterprise. As leaders, you have a vested interest in the success of your employees. You want them to succeed because they will help you succeed. The surest way to guarantee their success is to create the environment and programs that ensure the fullest development of their potential. This development of the abilities and skills of employees is an ongoing process requiring your continual interest and active participation.

Methods of Training

Training is a multi-faceted process that aims to teach employees all of the necessary knowledge, skills, and abilities to perform their jobs properly. However, training cannot be done in any systematic or consistent way until you have defined standards, policies, and procedures, and, most importantly for consistency sake, put them in writing. While this process is time-consuming and laborious, it forces you to define the quality you are trying to achieve.

Fortunately for most businesses, there is a great deal of material available that describes procedures for being a sales clerk, a cashier, a waiter, etc. In most cases, you'll want to customize the material to your own needs, but at least you won't have to start from scratch. Training material must be formatted in ways that make the information easy to absorb. These can be in the form of orientations, self-study workbooks, short classes given by leaders on an ongoing basis, checklists for repetitive tasks, scripting and role-playing of critical customer interfaces, diagrams, charts, or any combination of these that makes it easy for you to train and your employees to understand.

Finally, training material will change over time reflecting the realities of your business. Encourage your employees to give you feedback on the adequacy of their training. They deal directly with customers and can readily tell you what does and doesn't work, what customers do and don't respond to. This feedback should be used to constantly refine your training material.

Given the evolutionary nature and volume of training material, it makes sense to keep your material in an electronic format. If you have access to a personal computer, put your training material in a word processing program. If you don't have a PC, get one, either through your company or by purchasing one for your own use. The skills you develop in using a PC and standard word processing, spreadsheet, and database software will be invaluable to you as your career progresses.

Responsibility for Training

Some companies have centrally-administered training programs supporting their operations. Despite the existence and quality of this support, supervisors are ultimately responsible for ensuring that employees are properly trained.

Formal training is only part of the process. You must provide workplace orientations and detailed job training for new employees, observe their ongoing performance, and make on-the-spot corrections. Periodic meetings with employees for refresher training are also part of your ongoing training responsibilities.

Do not allow poorly trained employees to train new employees. Departmental trainers may be used, but the process must be formalized and closely supervised.

Practice Delegation

Delegation can be a tremendous training tool for talented individuals who want to learn and do more. Consider the following:

Melinda was hired as a temporary administrative assistant to help open an upscale, private golf club. I expected that we would need her for less than six months, but she quickly demonstrated extraordinary abilities. She showed tremendous initiative in tackling assignment after assignment; she showed great attention to the many details we faced; she was unafraid to make decisions; and, she had a knack for working with and supervising others.

As I became busier and busier, I began to rely on Melinda more and more. Delegating to her was easy because I always knew she would do an outstanding job. Within months she was supervising housekeeping and maintenance, establishing standards and policy, dealing with member issues, and attending various committee meetings.

Based upon her value to the team, I promoted her to Clubhouse Manager later that year. Her efforts and contribution were evident to all who knew her. Looking back on that challenging time, I can honestly say that I could not have done it without her. The next year, our management company offered Melinda her own club. In less than two years she had progressed from a temporary administrative assistant to General Manager of a prestigious private club.

While Melinda was always gracious in crediting me for her rapid rise, I will attest that the mentoring process went both ways. I will always be grateful for the many hours of hard work she spared me during the opening of that club, as well as the opportunity to observe first-hand her talent for directing others while gaining and maintaining their trust, respect, and dedicated efforts.

Delegating duties to employees makes sense for three reasons:

◆ It frees up your time for other matters,

◆ It develops employees to take on broader responsibilities, and

◆ It prepares others to step into your position should you move on.

Practice delegation by selecting one or more employees who show both the aptitude and the interest to take on expanded duties. Your role towards these individuals should be that of a mentor.

When mentoring staff, in addition to showing them what to do, you need to explain in depth the reasons behind various duties. If they are to grow into broader responsibilities, they will need to have knowledge, not just technical experience. While mentoring can be time-consuming, it will ultimately free up your time. Your employees will appreciate both the interest and effort devoted to their development, and your career and personal development will be advanced by the additional time you have to focus on other issues and projects.

Be aware that:

◆ Unless you make a concerted effort to provide employees proper direction, feedback, and ongoing growth opportunities, delegating may alienate them. In other words, don't use them. You need to put effort into their growth and make it worthwhile for them as well as for you.

◆ If you put employees in a supervisory role, pay close attention to how they interact with other staff. The critical aspects of supervision are directing and motivating employees. Many first-time supervisors have difficulty with the more subtle aspects of directing employees and may end up alienating the rest of the team.

◆ When you delegate the authority to do something to a subordinate, you still retain the responsibility that it is done correctly. Never use the excuse that you told a subordinate to do something and he or she didn't do it.

Delegating requires extra effort on the part of a leader, but ultimately it is one of the most rewarding things you can do. Not only will you have more time to concentrate on projects and details, but you also help others grow personally and professionally – certainly a win-win scenario for everyone.

Communicating with Employees

Communication

People have a great need for information, particularly when it pertains to them and their environment. In the absence of information, people fear the worst. Employees who are informed about the goals and direction of their company are better able to contribute to its success.

As a leader you possess a great deal of information about the company. You attend meetings where goals, problems, projects, and other operational details are discussed. Much of this information should be communicated to employees. Seldom is there a reason to keep them in the dark.

When leaders become absorbed in their own sense of urgency about plans, projects, and priorities, it is easy to forget that employees lack this valuable information. To foster this same sense of urgency in employees, communicate the details of such planning when appropriate.

Develop the habit and the systems to constantly communicate with employees. While memos and written material help, periodic departmental meetings allow dialogue and give employees an opportunity to ask questions and express concerns.

Every day you talk to one or more of your employees. Use these conversations to paint the vision, explain the big picture, and connect the small daily task to the larger goal. The extra few minutes spent doing this pays immense dividends in employee commitment. The trust, confidence, rapport, and self esteem engendered by such communication will become a driving force of energy and enthusiasm within your enterprise.

Communicating is a complex process. We communicate not only with words, but also with facial expressions, body language, and tone of voice. Words themselves are imprecise and subject to many interpretations. Some words have different shades of meaning. "Tenacious" has a totally different connotation than "stubborn," and to describe employees as "hard working" is very different from calling them "workaholics."

There are also cultural differences, differing educational levels, varied work backgrounds, and diverse life experiences. Listeners filter everything you say through their biases and predispositions, frequently choosing to hear what they want to hear or what they already believe. Finally, communication usually gets garbled as it is passed on.

What all this means is that you cannot take communication for granted. Never assume that someone has understood. It is too easy to be misunderstood. The following points will help improve communications:

◆ Be up front with your employees. Tell them what your expectations and perceptions are and that it's their responsibility to influence your perceptions about their performance.

◆ Information provided in managers' meetings must be passed to employees. Ensure that information is being passed and understood. Routinely ask employees if they know what information was disseminated at meetings.

◆ When you make decisions or implement plans, communicate them to everyone directly involved and to other affected areas of the company to prevent things from falling through the cracks.

◆ Have employees repeat important instructions back to you to ensure they have understood.

◆ Encourage employee feedback. Communication is a two-way street. It must flow up as well as down. Your employees need to hear from you and you need to hear from them.

◆ Some communications are so important they must be put in writing. If you communicate in writing, write out the message and sit on it for awhile, then reread it before it's issued. Soft-pedal the tone of written communications, including e-mail messages. Since recipients can't see your face or hear your voice, the message may come across with unintended harshness.

◆ Documentation fosters continuity. When key people leave a company and take their knowledge with them, the enterprise suffers. Put your standards, policies, and procedures in writing so that they are widely understood and passed on properly. Each operational area should have desktop policy and procedure manuals that are periodically updated.

Closure on Issues

Solving problems is a major function of leaders. Every day new problems crop up and, if not addressed, threaten the smooth functioning of the company. Simply talking about problems doesn't solve them. If so, complaining would be a highly valued professional skill.

Leaders must prioritize problems, addressing the more significant ones first. To solve a problem, the causes and underlying issues must be sought out, alternative solutions explored, discussions with other affected departments held, and finally, a DECISION MUST BE MADE. Even then, the solution is not complete until employees have been informed of the decision and changes have been completely implemented.

Carolyn joined our four-star desert resort as Guest Services Manager. She came highly recommended and made an immediate impact on the operation. She was instrumental in advocating and purchasing a new computerized front office system that stream-lined reservations, check-in, and housekeeping.

She worked long hours to make the installation a success, always scheduled herself to work on busy days, and was unfailingly pleasant to guests. Seeing Carolyn's smiling face behind the desk always gave me great comfort in knowing that everything was in good hands.

In time, I began to hear grumbling from Carolyn's staff, noticed an increase in departmental absenteeism, and fielded frequent guest complaints about the inefficiency of the desk staff when she was off. In a closed-door meeting requested by her staff, I discovered that Carolyn had ignored complaints about lack of proper training and problems with the system.

Since the new systems and procedures came easily to her, Carolyn dismissed the challenges her employees found in the system, claiming that they were "just stupid." In speaking with her about the situation, Carolyn grew defensive, blamed her staff for attitude problems, and was particularly angry that they had come to me.

Instead of keeping open lines of communication with her employees and following through to ensure complete implementation, she shut off their legitimate concerns about the system. Instead of anticipating and working through the problems associated with this major change, Carolyn saw every problem raised as a criticism of her decision to implement the new system. Rather than enlisting the help of her staff to solve the problems, she chose to cast them as adversaries to her success.

Any major change, no matter how well planned and executed, will present ongoing challenges. Until employees are thoroughly trained and become used to new systems and procedures, there will be difficulties. While much research and effort went into the purchase of the new system, for Carolyn the real work commenced with the installation.

This was the time to ensure open lines of communication, to listen to employee concerns, and to address their problems, real and perceived. Whatever problems came up, Carolyn should have addressed them with an open mind, planned and implemented solutions, and communicated thoroughly with her employees. Until there was full closure on all issues, there was potential for further turmoil.

No matter what problems or issues are raised, employees deserve a response. Closure is often a simple matter of getting back to them to let them know that their concerns will be addressed. Even if you decide not to take action, you owe it to them to let them know that decision. If you don't, they have no way of knowing whether you forgot or you don't care.

Positive Feedback

Since leaders focus on solving problems, it is natural to concentrate on the problem areas of an operation. But in your effort to fix what is wrong don't forget to recognize all that is right.

There are seldom opportunities for dramatic heroism in most businesses. However, there are the daily, dedicated efforts of employees faced with monotonous routine, difficult situations inherent in customer service, and detail, detail, detail. Employees should be recognized for the quiet, unprepossessing heroism that this involves. Simply put, do not forget to thank your employees for the good things they do every day – it probably outweighs the bad 50 to 1.

"Open Door" versus "Open Mind" Policy

An "Open Door' policy means you are accessible to your employees who have questions and problems. Such a policy will not work, no matter what it is called, if your employees do not perceive a genuine commitment to listening and problem-solving. The difference between an "Open Door" and an "Open Mind" policy is the attitude and commitment of the leader.

An "Open Mind" policy helps to uncover problems in your operation, defuses potential blow-ups, builds trust, and improves communication. To be successful with an "Open Mind" policy, you must:

◆ Be available, accessible, and approachable.
◆ Listen. Let employees speak. Be patient and constructive in listening to concerns and offering help.
◆ Be fair and consistent.
◆ Be prepared to get involved and follow through to solve problems.
◆ Ensure closure on issues.

If you are concerned about being overwhelmed by employees coming forward, set some guidelines such as "by appointment only" or "as time permits." If some employees are abusing an open door, be forthright and tell them to take greater responsibility in solving their own problems.

Two points of caution:

◆ While making yourself accessible to employees with problems, keep the interests of the company foremost in mind. This means not becoming an enabler for a problem employee or spending too much time assisting one employee to the detriment of the organization.

◆ Don't get emotionally involved in the affairs of your employees, and don't offer advice regarding their personal lives. Instead, refer them to professionals who are trained to help individuals with personal, emotional, and mental health issues.

Motivating Employees

Motivation and Morale

Employee turnover rates, employee attitudes, body language, and facial expressions speak volumes about a company. The signs are easy to see – grumbling, fearfulness, under-breath comments, lack of humor or gallows humor, cynical signs on desks or screen savers, and sour, negative attitudes.

Poor morale comes from poor leaders. Employees are not to blame. They are simply responding to a lack of leadership. Poor morale is solved by a genuine interest in the welfare of employees, trust, constant feedback, good two-way communications, clear goals, and positive motivation.

Leaders must motivate their employees to do what needs to be done, not just to get by, but to excel. Leaders are vitally concerned about their employees' morale. Poor morale can cripple the effectiveness of any group of people.

You must set the example and be positive and upbeat. Bad moods can destroy an organization, especially if it is yours. It is your responsibility to keep your employees up. Don't tolerate sour, negative attitudes. Unless you put a stop to them, they will grow like a cancer and be just as destructive.

A vivid memory of mine is of working at a historic hotel where the controller had been "in residence" for over twenty years. Martha never smiled, and she seemingly despised hotel guests, vendors, and other employees. Her isolation, constant grumbling, and obvious contempt for all around her poisoned the day-to-day atmosphere of the operation.

Staff social functions were occasions for Martha to complain about others who had not done their part or had performed poorly. Staff meetings always included diatribes on how planned improvements were pointless because guests always complained and employees didn't care. Despite her critical and central role in the operation, other employees avoided her like the plague since she was so unpleasant. Naturally this led to all sorts of problems, lack of cooperation, and miscommunication.

Finally, after much fruitless counseling and despite her longevity, we fired Martha. The new controller we hired placed great emphasis on being part of the team, meeting with other department heads to explore their concerns and issues, and making a positive contribution to planning and change.

Morale improved immediately. Line employees and managers seemed to have a new enthusiasm for the challenges we faced. Cooperation and consideration became the order of the day. As we gathered steam, improvements in the operation were readily apparent, and we all took pride in our efforts and accomplishments.

Even our regular guests noticed the new attitude and complimented us on our many initiatives.

I expected things to improve without Martha's ill humor, yet I was stunned by the difference her departure made. It seems her negativity impacted many on the staff. The collective emotional energy invested in dealing with her was put to better use and everyone was better for it.

While you can't control the mood swings of others, you can expect and require your employees to treat their fellow employees with courtesy and respect. You can insist on a cheerful and positive attitude. Any employee who refuses to make this basic commitment to the group welfare should seek other employment or, if suffering from a medical condition or emotional problem, seek professional help.

In dealing with many issues of motivation and morale, a little sincere human concern goes a long way. The people who work for you are like you, basically good-at-heart, each with his or her own strengths and weaknesses. Be gentle and nurturing and give them the benefit of the doubt. Show understanding in helping and teaching them. Yet be uncompromising and fanatical in your dedication to right attitude and quality of service.

Make employees part of the team, remembering that you are their coach. Share ideas with them, brainstorm with them, and listen to their ideas. A person with a stake in an organization has a greater sense of commitment.

A little praise and recognition goes a long way in building morale and esprit. If employees bring you good ideas, make sure they get recognition for their contribution. Never, ever take credit for an employee's idea. Your superiors will be far more impressed by your self-confidence and generosity of spirit in giving credit where it is truly due. Conversely, nothing will destroy your standing with employees faster than claiming credit for their accomplishments and ideas.

Know and address your employees by name. Meet with your employees frequently, both formally and informally. Talk to them every day. Ask for problems; hound them for problems. If they honestly believe you will try to solve the problems they face, they will open up.

Painting the Vision

As a leader you must have a vision of what you are trying to achieve with your operation. If you have no vision of what you want your operation to be, how it is to function, or what quality of work your employees will produce, you are merely maintaining the status quo and are providing little value to your company.

Vision is useless if not shared. Talk about it day in and day out. Vision should be so ingrained in the work lives of your employees that it is constantly on their minds. When it is, all of their abilities and efforts are directed by and toward it.

Goal Setting

Have goals for your service team. While each leader often operates from goals that are unstated, it is far better to share them with employees. This way, every employee can assist in working toward goals.

Many companies have a strategic plan that outlines long-range goals. Using these organizational goals for guidance, develop and communicate team goals, giving employees an opportunity to ask questions and seek clarification.

You may want to establish individual goals for employees that include their input or feedback to foster a sense of ownership. This can be done during performance evaluations. Not only do you review employees' past performance, but you also establish targets or achievements for them to aim for in the coming period.

Once goals have been established, constantly reiterate them and provide feedback to employees regarding their efforts to achieve them. Most people want to participate in a larger effort and know how their daily efforts are contributing. Like successful athletic coaches, leaders who routinely "cheerlead" staff understand the immense energies that can be marshaled to a cause.

Handshakes and High Fives

A simple yet effective way of cementing work relationships is to shake employees' hands. Politicians understand the value of "pressing the flesh." A variation on this traditional practice is the "high five" used by athletes. Psychologically, this touching of others establishes contact and rapport. While gratuitously touching employees is inappropriate, the hand-shake is an accepted sign of recognition and respect.

A hearty handshake of greeting each day, as well as using the opportunity at the end of the work shift to thank employees for their efforts, is a marvelously simple way of establishing a bond with your employees. As with any other symbol of relationship, the handshake must be sincere, open, and direct. There can be no question of ulterior motive, only good fellowship and cheer. Phoniness is evident to everyone.

Summary

How employees are treated has a direct bearing on how your customers are treated.

Understand and apply the "Principles of Employee Relations."

Know how to direct your employees so that you elicit their best work and avoid the pitfalls of poor supervision.

You are responsible for training employees. Training must cover the details of company standards, policies, and procedure.

Written training material will ensure consistency.

Delegation requires effort on a leader's part, but ultimately frees up your time for other things.

Good two-way communication will help foster understanding and a sense of teamwork.

Never underestimate the role of good morale within your service team. Leaders are responsible for motivation and morale.

Serving Your Customers

It makes no difference whether you call them customers, clients, patrons, guests, or members – the bottom line for all your leadership efforts is customer satisfaction. Ultimately, these are the people who pay your wages. Continued patronage ensures your company's success.

As a supervisor you have some contact with customers because you are a working leader, but it is the employees of your service team who handle the bulk of your customer contacts. Set the standard for your employees by your behavior towards customers.

Think Customers First!

Your perceptions mean nothing in your dealings with customers. Only the customers' perceptions count. Every complaint must be treated as legitimate and real – as it is to the customer!

Simply because you don't receive complaints, doesn't mean customers are happy. Many just go away disappointed or mad. You must constantly seek their feedback and then act on it. Only in this way will your customers know that you are genuinely interested in their patronage.

Never disparage customers. This sets a bad example for employees, creates and reinforces a "we versus they" mentality, and may be overheard by customers – in any case, it does not reflect well on you or the company.

Just as importantly, neither you nor your employees should ever complain to customers about your employer, your workplace, its policies and procedures, or internal events and actions. When you do, you act unprofessionally and diminish yourself and your place of business in the eyes of the customer.

A Service Ethic

In today's society many of the conventions that marked social intercourse in the past are seen as outmoded. Yet civility, good manners, and a desire to be of service to others remain important qualities of civilized life. This is particularly so in situations where you are seeking the goodwill of others.

The need to attract and retain customers has given rise to the term "service profession" to classify those who work in jobs whose primary purpose is to serve customers. But what does it mean to be in the "service profession"?

A traditional approach would be to consider those who work in a service profession as servants. For the time they are being served, customers are temporarily one's superiors and should be deferred to as a sign of respect.

While this approach is technically correct, the word "servant" does not sit well with most of us. Other titles such as "associate," "server," "wait staff," "host," and "assistant" are widely used to denote service employees. Whether these titles convey the appropriate attitude required for quality service is open to debate, and ultimately that debate is immaterial.

Service employees are people who choose to serve other people as a means of earning a living. What they are called is unimportant as long as they are not offended by it and they are imbued with a strong service ethic.

Establishing and maintaining this ethic is the shared responsibility of the company and the supervisor. The company establishes its standards of service, but it is up to the supervisor to teach employees what is expected and to hold them accountable for their performance and behavior.

Service standards are much more than just the technical aspects of delivering service; they encompass employees' attitudes and sensitivity to the needs and desires of the customer. Teaching these more abstract standards to employees is at the heart of establishing a strong service ethic.

The following and similar points should be stressed to all employees to help them understand the appropriate service ethic. Make sure they understand why they should:

◆ Step aside when approached by customers on walkways, on stairs, and in hallways. Even if there is sufficient room to pass, employees should make a point of moving aside as a sign of deference and respect.

◆ Talk quietly when customers are present. Employees shouldn't carry on personal conversations in dining areas, lobbies, hallways, retail spaces, or other public areas of your operation.

◆ Interrupt personal conversations at the approach of customers. Giving them immediate attention demonstrates respect and dedication to their comfort and welfare. Not giving immediate attention can be perceived as a subtle way of putting customers in "their place." This is unacceptable and damaging behavior in any business.

◆ Be discreet in their personal habits. A customer should never see employees eating, drinking beverages, or smoking. These interfere with an immediate and absolute focus on the customer. Even if they don't interfere, they give a negative impression – and impressions are what service is all about!

◆ Be formal when interacting with customers. For employees to assume familiarity with customers is to presume equality with them. In the service profession employees willingly assume a service position and should not presume anything in their dealings with customers.

◆ Talk slowly and deliberately using standard English usage when speaking with customers. Employees should avoid slang expressions or trade jargon. A customer may or may not know what is meant when a menu item is said to be "eighty-sixed." Employees should never call customers "you guys" as in, "How are you guys doing tonight?"

◆ Be aware of body language. Employees should not lean against walls, sit on furniture in public areas, stand with hands on hips or in pockets, or with arms folded across their chests. These convey the attitude that the facility belongs to them. This may seem like nitpicking detail, but these signals send powerful messages to customers.

◆ Be knowledgeable about their jobs and what is expected of them. Employees should take it upon themselves to learn everything they can about the business. This also means supervisors must do a thorough job of training employees.

◆ Make every effort to understand customers' perspectives. Every problem customers perceive is a real and immediate problem for them. To solve it, employees need to focus their attention and listen carefully to what is actually being said. They should not assume they know what the problem is.

◆ Recognize that some customers will try to take advantage, but the majority have legitimate concerns. Employees should understand that there will always be "high maintenance" customers. Satisfying their higher expectations is part of the cost of doing business and the ultimate challenge of service. So employees should not dwell on the difficult few; rather, they must recognize each request or complaint as legitimate and focus on the solution.

◆ Understand that customer complaints are not personal unless they make them so by becoming defensive. The real issue is not the problem that led to the complaint; what matters is resolving it quickly, cheerfully, and gracefully. Employees should always offer a sincere apology as they are doing so.

◆ Make everything about the operation and facility as plain, simple, and clear as possible for the customer. Employees may know where the rest rooms and lounge are, but is it as clear to a customer who has never visited before? To be as helpful as possible, employees should consider that nothing about the operation or its services is clear or simple to a first-time customer.

It is a supervisor's responsibility to ensure that employees are thoroughly familiar with the company's service ethic. It is also imperative that you are seen to consistently practice these requirements yourself.

A Service Attitude

One of my first line supervisors was a banquet manager at a large metropolitan hotel. Ben was older, had a large family, and was a proud and loving father. Despite his busy life, he always had time for his guests and his large banquet staff, whom he treated like family.

Though he supervised over fifty people, he not only knew us all by name, but he was aware of our individual circumstances – if we were students, where we lived, what we did in our spare time. By taking the time to know each of us as individuals, he was able to connect with us in ways few other managers could.

For over a year, I watched him deal with guests, hotel management, and a large, boisterous, and diverse staff. He made those of us who worked for him understand that service is not just a part-time pursuit – it's a way of life.

It was obvious that Ben was universally respected by all who knew him. I had seen him greet many dignitaries and celebrities by name and was even amazed to see a U.S. Senator stop by to say hello to him.

When Ben died a couple of years ago, more than three hundred people attended his funeral. He was eulogized with warmth, humor, and emotion. The clear lesson I learned from this great man was that the love he put into service was returned to him a hundredfold.

While each person brings his or her own attitudes to the workplace, your company expects employees to be indoctrinated into a culture of absolute dedication to quality and the needs of the customer.

Your emphasis as a leader and all the training focus for your employees is on learning how to say YES to customers. If this attitude is kept foremost in mind, it will help you and your employees handle any unusual requests or difficult situations involving customers. This indoctrination is the ongoing responsibility of leaders at every level and can best be accomplished by your wholehearted support, daily reinforcement, and personal example.

Equally important, this attitude should characterize your work relationships with fellow employees – your internal customers. Everyone who works for your company is a member of a team trying to accomplish the same mission. Cheerful and complete cooperation with one another makes work easier, more meaningful, and fun. Your first thought when approached by a customer, external or internal, should be "How can I help this person; how can I be of service?"

Attitude is the major determinant of success in any endeavor. Your thoughts color everything you do. Each person has a filter through which all sense perceptions pass. Since the conscious mind can only process so much information, perceptions are screened and only those supporting your thought system, biases, and views are accepted. All others are rejected. Stated another way – since your brain interprets sensory information to support what you already believe – YOU ARE WHAT YOU THINK!

If you believe yourself to be misunderstood or mistreated, you will seek every piece of evidence to support this belief. If you are optimistic and happy, you will select every perception that supports that happiness and optimism.

The process is self-reinforcing and reciprocal. If your thoughts tend to the negative, you will see only the negative. If a person is a liar, he or she will assume that everyone lies and will go through life never trusting anyone.

The implication is that you create the world you want through your thoughts. People who are upbeat and look for the good in everything know that, while they cannot control events, THEY CAN CONTROL THEIR REACTIONS TO THOSE EVENTS! Simply put, you can make whatever you want of any situation.

Attitudes are clearly infectious and you owe it to others to be as positive and cheerful as possible. One defeatist, grumbling, negative attitude can ruin the day for many others. The sad thing is that you allow the negative person to do this. When one considers the uproar in society over the danger to people's health from passive smoking, it is surprising that they aren't just as adamant about the threat to health from passive bad attitude.

So don't tolerate your employees' bad moods. Confront them; shock them back into an acceptable frame of mind. Tell them to go home if they can't be in a better mood.

The requirement must be:

"Be of Good Cheer or Don't Be Here!"

As a leader you are responsible for building morale within your team. Protect your employees from people with negative attitudes and sour moods. Don't permit one employee to drag down an entire operation. Confront, counsel, and, if necessary, terminate the employee.

Creating Enthusiasm

Work is a major part of everyone's life. It should be an integral part. Most people work from necessity. They exchange labor and time for wages to support themselves, their families, and their lifestyles. Some people see this exchanged labor and time as something apart from themselves, a necessary evil to be borne with as little commitment and effort as possible. Such people are alienated from their work.

Unfortunately, too many people suffer this alienation. They view work as an unpleasant means to an end – merely a job to make money. They are disengaged from their labors. They don't realize that every moment of hating and feeling miserable about their work is a moment of hating and feeling miserable about their lives and, ultimately, themselves.

But people have a choice. They can either quit the job they hate or, if that's not possible, they can attempt to change their minds about their work. By viewing it as an integral part of their lives – not separate from living – and focusing on the quality of their time at work, people can truly restore a lost portion of their lives.

In the service profession, you can engage with your work by focusing your efforts on the comfort, satisfaction, and well-being of every customer. This focusing – concentration if you will – is very much akin to the Zen idea of total involvement; that is, one's actions and work are not separate and apart from the process of living. In the final analysis, to do anything well, including work, is to live well.

By developing enthusiasm in your employees and teaching them to look at service to the customer in a positive way, you can help them joyfully accept the challenge of making the experience of others a better one. Not only will they get the satisfaction of a job well done, but also the experience and pleasure of giving to others.

How Best to Serve Customers

While this chapter is entitled "Serving Your Customers," notice that all of the advice relates to your employees, what they must do, how they must act, and their motivation, morale, and enthusiasm.

This underscores the important point that it is your employees who provide the service. Your role as the supervisor is to "serve" your employees by being an effective leader and providing the necessary training, direction, and ongoing support so that they may do their jobs better.

Summary

The bottom line of all your leadership efforts is customer satisfaction.

Customers define problems; you solve them.

Never disparage customers.

Do not complain about your company or workplace to customers.

What service employees are called is not important so long as it doesn't offend, and they are imbued with a strong service ethic.

The service ethic is a shared responsibility of the company and the supervisor.

A service ethic is more than the techniques of providing service; it encompasses the leader's attitude and sensitivity to the needs and desires of customers. Supervisors must teach employees these more abstract standards.

Employees must be indoctrinated into the company's culture of quality and service.

You and your employees must learn how to say YES to both your external and internal customers.

Since your mind screens sense perception, reinforcing what it already believes, YOU ARE WHAT YOU THINK!

While you cannot control events that happen to you, YOU CAN CONTROL YOUR REACTION TO THOSE EVENTS!

Attitudes are infectious. Don't tolerate employees with bad moods. Your requirement must be, "BE OF GOOD CHEER OR DON'T BE HERE!"

Help employees improve performance and enrich their own lives by developing positive attitudes about work.

Serving Your Shareholders

Who are Shareholders?

Whether a company is privately or publicly owned, the shareholders are the owners of the enterprise. They have invested their money in the venture with the expectation of receiving a return on their investment. Without shareholders and their willingness to assume risks, you and your team would not have a job.

Often a company's shareholders are removed from the operation. They allow professional managers to run the day-to-day business of the company. But even if they are seldom or never on the premises, this does not mean that they do not have needs to be met.

While you may have little opportunity to directly serve shareholders, everything you do to serve the company's customers and everything you do to better organize and operate the enterprise does have a direct bearing on satisfying your shareholders.

Shareholders' Needs

Shareholders have a number of expectations for the performance of their business. If you do a good job taking care of your employees and customers, it will be easier to satisfy the needs of your shareholders. These needs fall into several broad categories:

Pride of ownership. Shareholders derive prestige and satisfaction from the success of their company and that success is directly attributable to the quality and efficiency of operations. Your leadership has a direct bearing on this quality and efficiency.

Return on Investment. Capital is the dynamo that drives a business. It takes money to renovate a restaurant, to launch a new product line or service, to purchase inventories, to hire new employees, and to expand operations. Shareholders expect a return on their investment of capital.

Asset protection. Shareholders expect that the leaders of the company will safeguard their assets. This includes cash, invested funds, change and petty cash funds, inventories, furniture, fixtures, equipment, facilities, vehicles, and the name, goodwill, and reputation of the company. Leaders cannot fully safeguard a company's assets without the willing assistance and commitment of their employees.

Professionally-operated "going concern." A primary responsibility to shareholders is to operate the business responsibly and professionally as a "going concern," that is, as a business that intends to stay in business.

Ensuring Pride of Ownership

Shareholders take pride in their ownership of a company. They want the company to be successful and to have standing. This is true whether the company is local or global.

Usually, the smaller the company, the greater the owner's personal stake in the company's reputation. Often in small businesses the owner's reputation is synonymous with a company's standing.

But whether large or small, it is important that employees faithfully and professionally represent their company. Unseemly, unsavory, or unprofessional conduct on the part of employees, whether on or off the job, can damage a company's standing and discredit its owners or shareholders.

On the other hand, establishing and maintaining the company's reputation for integrity, product quality, and customer service gives owners and shareholders cause for pride. It is here that you, as a supervisor, can make a difference.

In leading your service team, you have both the opportunity and the responsibility to indoctrinate your staff in the importance of the impressions they make on people in general and your customers in particular. Friendly, outgoing, courteous, and consistent service will cause customers to sing your company's praises to everyone they meet. It is also important that your leadership efforts focus on establishing and maintaining consistent quality and service.

Establishing Quality

Each area of your operation should have defined standards of quality. Once established, these standards must become second nature to everyone. As a supervisor you should constantly be looking for ways to improve the standard or ways to alleviate problems for customers and employees. This is often difficult to do for someone who is immersed in the operation.

One way is to listen carefully to your customers and employees. In the case of customers, the indirect communication of their buying habits can speak volumes about their perception of your business and its problems. Carefully tracking your operation's sales, sales mix, traffic patterns, and other indicators of customer preference will help you and your team better understand their desires and needs.

Another way to improve your standards is to ask other leaders to come in and look at your area with a fresh eye. Sometimes, it is surprising how obvious problems can be to someone who doesn't deal with them every day.

Ongoing feedback from your employees will help you better understand the needs and desires of customers. Since employees have the most contact with customers, they are in the best position to provide this information. Something as simple as an employee overhearing and reporting a customer comment can be used by your team to improve product or service.

Responsibility for Quality Control

The responsibility for meeting standards rests solely with you. Establish a number of means, including quality assurance checklists, benchmarks of key operating statistics, and inspections to monitor adherence to standards. Leaders at all levels should aggressively monitor operations to ensure quality standards are maintained.

Walk around your areas of responsibility on a daily basis, checking that everything is being done to standards. As mentioned before, this checking sends powerful signals to your team about what you consider important.

Importance of Marketing

Marketing, plain and simple, is selling one's product or service. But you can't credibly sell products and services without selling yourself. Believe in yourself and what you are doing as well as the products and services your company offers.

Make a point of meeting your customers. Get out from your workspace and introduce yourself to your regulars. Make a habit of talking to customers daily. Make small-talk, compliment them on their clothes, their children, or anything that is appropriate. Make an effort to remember their names. Establish a bond – the connection that makes them want to come back and to speak well of you and your company.

Most decisions a company makes have marketing implications. Pricing, packaging, convenience, service, attention to detail, and attention to customers – all have a direct and major impact on marketing the enterprise.

Companies spend a significant amount of money trying to market their products and services. Despite this outlay one bad customer experience can ruin everyone's best efforts. Conversely, word-of-mouth advertising is the best and cheapest form of advertising you can get, but you have to earn it.

Constantly reinforce these simple truths to your employees. Eastern Airlines said it best, when they said, "We have to earn our wings every day." As in any service organization, you are only as good as your last customer contact.

Organization, Order, Cleanliness, & Maintenance

Organization, order, cleanliness, and maintenance, both in public view and behind the scenes, are accurate indicators of the quality of your operation and your attention to detail. Ensure that your operation and work areas are well organized, are maintained in an orderly state, and have the highest standards of cleanliness and maintenance.

Shortly after becoming General Manager of my first hotel, Rachel, our ever-energetic Executive Housekeeper, took me on a tour of various storage areas, including a crawl space under one of the wings of the hotel. Each was crammed full of old hotel furnishings, equipment, and other "junk" that had accumulated over the years. Most of the items were in bad shape, made worse by years of storage in unsuitable spaces.

Rachel pointed out that all of this stuff constituted a fire hazard, took up storage space that could be put to better use, and impeded her efforts to better organize her department. She suggested that we clear out all the junk and hold a "hotel sale." I appreciated her initiative and readily concurred.

It took a week to haul everything out into a tent, then inventory and tag it. Several weeks later we held the publicized sale. Believe it *or not, several hundred bargain-hunters showed up and we sold all but a handful of items, netting close to $10,000 for the hotel.*

While the $10,000 made a significant difference in our cash flow that month, the real benefit was to clear the hotel of unwanted items, which freed up space to better organize our storage areas and operation.

Countertops, cashier stations, front desks, and other workspaces where your customers interact with employees are windows into your operation. Keep them clean, neat, and uncluttered. I have often stepped up to cashier counters in restaurants only to be accosted by handwritten, dog-eared signs, yellowing newspaper items taped to walls, and notes to cashiers not to accept checks from various locals.

All of this is unnecessary and gives a negative impression of the operation. I can also say that the same carelessness that allows such clutter is a good indicator for the lack of quality of their food and service.

Ensuring Shareholders' Return on Investment

Having invested their money in an enterprise, share-holders expect a return on their investment. This means that the capital invested grows in value and is either returned in shareholder dividends or increases the value of the business – in either case, shareholders see the value of their investment increasing.

Meeting Budget

Every business has a budget, which is its financial plan for the coming period – usually a year. As a supervisor you are responsible for meeting your portion of the budget. The two major components of your budget are meeting or exceeding revenue expectations and controlling your costs.

As a leader you should be involved in the budgeting process and monitor actual performance versus the budget. Ongoing failure to meet budget must be corrected by bold intervention. Your job depends on it.

Meeting or Exceeding Revenue Expectations

Your service team can have a direct impact on your company's sales. Beyond the obvious correlation between outstanding service and repeat customers, your staff has daily opportunities to upsell products and services. You, as their leader, must train and motivate them to do so.

Part of the training and motivation is the need to share your goals with them. This is easily done by breaking down your budgeted sales into daily goals.

In one of the restaurants I was responsible for, the floor manager used a chalkboard in the service pantry to set daily goals for the number of meals served, the average check, alcoholic beverage sales, bottles of wine sold, and other daily revenue challenges. He also posted the month-to-date actual results compared to the budgeted numbers.

It was incredible to see how this simple technique galvanized the servers into action. Every day they checked their progress and there was a continual hum of interest and excitement about their efforts to beat "the numbers."

Next, the floor manager tied some simple awards into the process as further incentive. Not only did we continually exceed our revenue projections, but there was also a noticeable improvement in employees' attitudes and enthusiasm for the job.

Controlling Costs

Payroll cost is the single largest expense in most service organizations. Be aware of your payroll hours on a daily basis. Keep close control of overtime. Staff schedules must reflect forecasted levels of business.

There is a natural tendency to overstaff for the expected peaks of business. Because payroll is such a large part of your expense structure, plan to fill in during busy times, thereby maintaining service while controlling payroll costs.

In order to do this you must analyze the flow of your business to determine when you should be available to step in. By routinely checking your operations during traditionally busy periods, you can readily determine if your help is needed. When you are both willing and able to step in, you build camaraderie, morale, and loyalty among your employees; help control labor costs; and ensure consistent service to customers.

Another major cost that must be controlled is consumable items. This can be done by tracking usage rates for key items (high cost or high volume). Before you can do this, you have to identify items, organize storage areas, and specify stocking levels.

A high cost of goods sold may indicate a number of problems, but unless you validate your pricing periodically, there is a good chance that it is directly related to inappropriate pricing. Because of the volatility of ingredients, menu prices and portion sizes should be reviewed on an ongoing basis to assure the profit margin on each sale.

While menu items must be pre-costed and periodically verified, buffets and receptions should be post-costed on a periodic basis to ensure profitability. Sales mixes must be tracked and operating statistics benchmarked. Be familiar with your costs and look for ways to reduce them. Familiarity with these numbers must be routine and ongoing.

Review in detail a different area of expenditure every month so that you constantly update and review your cost structure. Make large expense categories your priority. Shop around for less expensive alternatives to high cost items.

Finally, manage your inventory levels closely. Large inventories may ensure that you never run out of stock, but they also lead to spoilage and pilferage while tying up capital that could be put to better use.

Financial and Statistical Analysis

Learn to read financial statements. Budgets should be based upon well-defined assumptions. Compare actual performance each month to the budget and analyze all significant variances.

Benchmark your operation. Benchmarking is the act of establishing a standard of performance based upon existing operating conditions.

I always make a point of benchmarking any new operation for which I assume responsibility. I do this with the understanding that I can only show my progress by benchmarking existing conditions. Then any improvements I make are evident to all. Consider the major league baseball player coming up for contract renegotiations. What does he use to make his case for a big-bucks increase in compensation?

Benchmarks are derived from measuring and tracking various operating statistics. Operating statistics can include anything you can measure – revenues, expenses, production processes, etc. Examples might be:

◆ Revenue statistics – measures of the volume of business such as meals served, rounds of golf, number of sales transactions. Also, the average customer expenditure such as average meal check, green fees per round, and average sale.

◆ Expense statistics – measures of labor cost such as payroll hours and average hourly wage. Also, measures of consumable supplies usage such as napkins used per meal served or laundry chemicals used per occupied guestroom.

◆ Production processes – measures of the speed, efficiency, or quality of procedures such as guest rooms cleaned per housekeeping payroll hour, inspection scores measuring the cleanliness of guest rooms, etc.

Benchmarks are significant in that they allow you to compare all future operations against the baseline standard. It also allows you to measure one operation against other similar operations or against the industry as a whole. Further, benchmarking allows you to spot emerging trends so you can make timely interventions.

Be meticulous and consistent in tracking operating statistics and be up-to-date and conversant with your numbers at all times. The time you spend tracking and analyzing your numbers of even incidental items will make you more knowledgeable about your operation.

While serving as Director of Operations for a small hotel chain, I was continually looking for ways to improve our operating efficiency. One of our hotel managers suggested that we establish a central warehouse for our seven properties. This warehouse allowed us to purchase in bulk, thereby saving money. The downside to the set-up, though, was the constant need to arrange delivery from the warehouse to the various properties in a three-state area.

The same manager recognized this drawback and established a procedure within her property to conduct monthly inventories of key items of guest supply. Each month she would send me a report showing the usage of approximately 20 items from her hotel.

By comparing the usage rates of bath soap and toilet paper with room-nights occupied at her property we were able to establish benchmark usage rates for these items which we used as a company-wide standard. For instance, her statistics showed that every room-night occupied consumed 1.21 bars of soap. This information was helpful in several ways.

Each year when we prepared the budgets, revenue projections were based upon our expectation of room-nights occupied at each hotel. With this information we were able to determine our soap needs month by month. It was then easy to negotiate with vendors to purchase a year's supply of soap for all hotels, but to have them "drop shipped" directly from the vendor's warehouse to our hotels on a quarterly basis. Not only were we able to negotiate a great price on the soap based on quantity, but we also didn't take up warehouse space with soap, nor did we have to deliver it to our hotels.

A further benefit occurred when I noticed that one of the hotels had a usage rate nearly double the other properties. Upon investigation, we found that their housekeepers were placing twice as much soap in each room than was specified in our standards. Quite expectedly, the guests were helping themselves to this "extra."

As you can see from this example, operating statistics can be significantly useful in monitoring and improving your operation. While there are as many statistics to track as your ingenuity and initiative allow, you should focus on key items and consider how easy or difficult it is to collect and track the numbers. Finally, the key to meaningful operating statistics is consistency in the methods of collection. Inconsistent statistics are useless for comparison purposes.

Protecting Shareholders' Assets

Safeguarding the company's assets begins with the leadership and integrity of its supervisors. First and foremost, you should set an unimpeachable example for your employees. If they see that you are careless with company property, that you take advantage of your position, that you appropriate company assets for personal use, that you are more concerned about your perquisites than the welfare of the company, they will find countless ways to do the same.

Make clear to your staff the connection between caring for your company's assets and the company's financial viability. They must understand that well-maintained equipment and facilities work better, need fewer costly repairs, and last longer, ensuring the success and longevity of the company and the jobs it provides.

Move quickly to repair damaged, inoperative, worn, or obsolete equipment and furnishings. By demonstrating the importance of keeping your facilities clean and well maintained, you not only serve your customers, but you also demonstrate to your staff the importance of caring for company assets.

Companies spend a great deal of money with public relations and marketing firms to ensure that products and services are looked upon favorably by customers and the general public. The name and good will of a company is looked upon as an asset and could affect the stock value of a company or the price paid for the company in a sale or merger. It is your responsibility and that of all your employees to protect this invaluable asset.

Put an end to petty pilferage. It is theft plain and simple. You can help by not tempting employees by allowing supplies and materials to be left all over the place. Warn employees of the consequences and then follow through whenever someone is caught snitching food from buffets, taking a roll of toilet paper or a trash bag. Leaders who permit an atmosphere where petty pilferage is allowed are not meeting their responsibilities and will themselves be held accountable.

Operating a Professional "Going Concern"

A "going concern" is a business that is operated to stay in business. The focus of such a company is on the future. Company executives have strategic plans for growth and expansion. The company is vitally concerned about societal trends, competitors, and threats to the company's future.

Such companies invest heavily in marketing the company and its products, in training their employees, and in the maintenance of facilities. Their intention is to not only stay in business, but to grow and prosper. Such companies recognize that the environment in which they operate is subject to flux and change.

Change in Business

Just as change is a constant in life, so it is in business. Enterprises and industries come and go. Some of the largest and most successful corporations in America are less than 30 years old. Many large and successful companies of our grandparents' time are gone.

In a highly dynamic and competitive environment, no company can prosper or survive long without changing. Why do businesses fail?

- ◆ They don't keep up with changing technology.
- ◆ In good times they assume higher costs that they are unable to shed quickly when the economy slows or sales drop off.
- ◆ They become complacent and fail to keep up with the changing wants and needs of their customers.
- ◆ They lose sight of their basic reasons for being in business.

◆ Their organizational structure becomes so compartmentalized and bureaucratic that it can't react quickly to changing circumstances or take advantage of opportunities. The process takes control of the operation and becomes primary.

Change should not be made just for the sake of change. It has to make sense financially and from a market standpoint. If it isn't broken, don't fix it. But if the numbers are down, something isn't working.

Leading Change

Amin came to work for me as the Restaurant Manager in an historic university-owned hotel. He faced many challenges, not the least of which was the fact that the restaurant was losing money and badly needed repositioning.

He attacked the problem with enthusiasm and energy, and he promptly ran into a buzz saw of opposition. It seems that many of his customers, including several academics who were powerful shapers of university opinion, thought the existing operation was just fine.

While surprised by their reaction to his plans, Amin developed a strategy to win them to his cause. He actively courted them, made appointments for office visits, listened to many nostalgic tales of meals gone by, but also heard in all the conversation their distinct desire to maintain the restaurant as a quiet, dignified place where ideas could be discussed over a good, reasonably-priced meal.

He then enlisted a respected professor's wife and interior designer with a deep sense of university tradition to prepare designs to renovate the restaurant. He also formed a focus group of key individuals to communicate menu preferences to the Chef. As the plans began to take shape he was careful to keep his many advisers abreast of developments.

Amin also took great pains to involve the food service staff in his planning and designs. Not only were their suggestions helpful, but they looked forward to the repositioning with proprietary interest.

Finally, the day came when the restaurant was closed for renovation. During the three-week closure, a number of our "advisers" stopped by to see how the project was coming. Most made reservations for re-opening day so they could bring friends and colleagues to see the results of "their work."

Needless to say, the re-opening was a great success. Certainly, there were some minor glitches, but the pride and good feeling of our many active participants carried the day.

As this example suggests, a lot of mistakes can be prevented if you take the time to completely think through the ramifications of planned changes. Attempt to understand the impact of proposed changes on all elements of the organization and customers alike.

Change can be threatening to employees. They sometimes do not understand that change can also be an opportunity. Reassure them. Much of how change is viewed is attitudinal and can be influenced by the manner in which you, as the leader, approach it.

Enact change in a manner that lessens the threat to employees. Lead your staff through change. Make sure they understand the reasons for the change and whatever new goals you have. Brief them thoroughly on new policies or procedures.

New processes also impact your customers, so make sure you communicate changes to them. Start well in advance of the proposed changes and "sell" new services and procedures to your customers.

Change isn't any good unless it works. Evaluate change and analyze the effectiveness of new systems, policies, and procedures. Corrections and modifications will inevitably be necessary. Do not be afraid to admit that things aren't going as planned or hoped. Intervene as necessary. Stay focused and committed until all the bugs are worked out.

Communicate well and thoroughly throughout the period of change. Fear feeds on itself and can get out of hand quickly. In the absence of information, employees will usually assume the worst. Listen to their fears and try to allay them.

A leader must exude confidence and enthusiasm for change. Be supportive of the change even if you don't agree with it. Leaders usually have opportunities to express disagreement with proposed changes. Once a decision is made, though, support the idea as if it were your own. Never disparage the change in front of your employees. You will doom it to failure.

Work to create an environment where change occurs naturally and the process of change thrives. It can be essential to your success.

How Best to Serve Shareholders

While all of the skills and initiatives in this chapter are the responsibility of supervisors, they can also belong to your service team. To the extent that you make your employees a part of your efforts, teach them, and share your goals and challenges with them, they will become willing helpers in your quest for quality and service.

Imagine the benefit of ten people trying to meet goals and budgets instead of one. Think of the natural enthusiasm that can be mustered when your benchmarks become theirs. Recognize the pride of accomplishment they will feel when the team not only meets, but exceeds expectations. This is truly a formula for success.

In simplest terms, when you serve your employees, they will serve your customers, who by their continued enthusiastic patronage will serve the needs of your shareholders.

The Pyramid of Successful Service depicts these relationships.

The Pyramid of Successful Service

Summary

Shareholders are the owners of your company.

Shareholders have certain expectations of company leaders:

Pride of ownership

♦ Ensure pride of ownership by faithfully and professionally representing your company through your personal integrity, product quality, and customer service.

♦ Leaders are responsible for establishing and maintaining the quality of their operations.

♦ Market yourself and your company to ensure success.

♦ Organization, order, cleanliness, and maintenance are accurate indicators of the quality of your operation.

Return on investment

◆ Ensure shareholders' return on investment by exceeding revenue projections and controlling costs.

◆ Since payroll cost is usually the single largest expense, controlling payroll cost is a priority for any leader.

◆ Benchmark your operation to track performance and spot trends.

Asset protection

◆ Protect your company's assets through your leadership and integrity, and by maintaining buildings, equipment, and furnishings.

◆ Put an end to petty pilferage.

Professionally-operated "going concern"

◆ Lead your operation as a business that intends on staying in business.

◆ Understand that change is a constant in business and that you must lead change.

You can best serve your shareholders by understanding that when you serve your employees, they serve your customers, who in turn serve the needs of your shareholders.

Leaders Beware!

There are certain actions on the part of supervisors that will cause problems for you and your company. The following ten basic guidelines will help you avoid problems and set the proper example for those you lead.

1. Consistency in all personnel actions

In today's litigious society it is essential that all personnel actions from screening interviews, to hiring, to providing opportunities for training and promotion, to counseling, disciplining, and terminating be consistent, fair, and professional.

Companies spend a great deal of time and energy defending themselves against formal complaints and lawsuits from employees claiming to have been treated unfairly or unprofessionally. In many cases, leaders who know and follow their company personnel policies, believe in the principles of employee relations, and act professionally can avoid these costly actions.

2. No retaliation

Employees have a right to come forward with their problems and concerns. While you may expect that they will come to you first, they may feel that you are part of the problem.

Should employees go over your head or file complaints against you, do not retaliate against them. The best way to avoid this is to have open communications with employees and be approachable for their problems and concerns.

The first question you should ask yourself when employees go outside the chain of command with their issues is why didn't they feel comfortable coming to you? This should be the cause of some serious soul-searching about your leadership, the level of trust you have built with your staff, and how well you communicate. Do not blame others for your failures.

Leaders who sincerely desire open and trusting relationships with their employees can use these episodes as valuable learning experiences.

3. No sexual harassment

Sexual harassment is defined as unwelcome sexual advances, requests for sexual favors, and other verbal or physical conduct of a sexual nature when:

◆ Submission to such conduct is made either explicitly or implicitly a term or condition of an individual's employment,

◆ Submission to or rejection of such conduct by an individual is used as the basis for employment decisions affecting the individual, or

◆ Such conduct has the purpose or the effect of interfering with an individual's work performance or creating an intimidating, hostile, or offensive working environment.

Sexual harassment is against the law, and it is the policy of most organizations that any incident of alleged sexual harassment be reported to management immediately. Allegations must be quickly and thoroughly investigated.

Most realize how emotionally charged this issue is. In many cases, the allegation can be as damaging as being found guilty. Therefore, be extremely careful how you treat your employees and avoid any words or actions that can be construed as being offensive or of a sexual nature.

4. No discriminatory practices

Biases, prejudice, disparaging remarks or jokes on the basis of race, creed, religion, gender, national origin, ethnic group, age, handicap, or sexual orientation cannot be tolerated. There is no place for bigotry or personal and cultural insensitivity in the workplace. While each person has his or her own biases and prejudices, do not let them interfere with your conduct and decisions as a leader. There are two good reasons for this:

◆ Senior management will usually deal swiftly with leaders who exhibit such behavior, and

◆ This behavior demeans people. It demeans those who do it and those who are subjected to it. Since your company is the sum of its parts, words or actions that attack the self esteem of any employee damage the company as a whole.

5. No favoritism

Scrupulously avoid any appearance of favoritism. The fact or perception of favoritism creates serious problems among employees. Many employee complaints stem from perceptions of unfairness on the part of leaders. Time, money, and energy is spent responding to these complaints, which takes away from the company's focus on customer service, improving operations, and planning.

In addition to the problems created for the organization as a whole, the perception of unfairness creates dissension and poor morale and destroys motivation within your work team.

6. No fraternization with employees

As a leader you must not, under any circumstances, enter into personal, intimate relations with employees under your direction.

Should you feel drawn to such a relationship, you must take steps to ensure that one or the other party in the relationship resigns his or her position. Just as nepotism creates problems in an organization, personal relationships can interfere with the performance of your official duties.

While some leaders may feel that they can carry on such a relationship without it affecting their professional judgment or duties, an intimate relationship with a subordinate is in itself evidence of compromised judgment.

7. No waste, fraud, or abuse

Abide by the highest ethical standards. If you cut corners and bend the rules when it comes to safeguarding the assets of the company, you can expect your employees will do likewise.

This is particularly important in regards to your personal productivity. Don't expect your employees to work hard if you don't set the example. Abuse any privilege associated with your position and risk the loss of your employees' respect.

Ethical standards are at the very heart of what you do – your personal and professional integrity. Often the appearance of wrongdoing can be as damaging as the reality. Follow the spirit as well as the letter of ethical requirements and set an unassailable example of conduct for those you lead and serve.

8. No disclosing confidential information

Never share confidential personnel or disciplinary information. What happens at the workplace should stay there. While it is impossible to control all the rumors and gossip circulating among staff, you can maintain confidentiality and not engage in this activity yourself.

Information about your company, such as financial statements, operating statistics, and internal problems should not be disclosed to persons or organizations external to your business. If a request for information seems legitimate, pass it on to your boss who will make the appropriate determination.

9. No complaining to employees

Leaders shoulder the burden of many responsibilities. When things are not going well, it is all too easy to seek out someone with whom to share the burden. This someone should never be one of your employees.

A major requirement of leaders is to possess the maturity to understand the potential negative consequences of confiding anxieties, doubts, and grievances to subordinates. Remember:

◆ You can have no expectation of confidentiality. What you say in these weak moments will most definitely be repeated.

◆ The friendly shoulder on which you unburden may not always be friendly.

◆ Your complaints undermine the respect you have built among staff and erode your authority.

◆ Your complaints may reflect poorly upon your boss or the company and can set up a conspiratorial "we versus they" situation. Obviously, this is not in anyone's best interest.

Avoid these consequences by maintaining a healthy professional distance between your employees and yourself. Treat them kindly, provide professional guidance, coach and cheerlead them, but studiously avoid sharing personal information or feelings with employees, for their sake as well as your own.

10. No favors from vendors

Frequently, supervisors will be offered favors and gifts by vendors. These may be in the form of seemingly small personal items, free products for personal use, gifts at holidays or on birthdays, tickets to concerts or sporting events, or invitations to parties to thank you for your patronage. While these may be genuine expressions of appreciation, they create problems for the leader.

Even in subtle ways they cloud your judgment, making it difficult to be truly objective in your purchasing decisions. Accepting even small favors starts you down a slippery path. At what point do you say no, when you have repeatedly said yes?

Finally, such favors create the appearance of compromise to everyone who is aware of them. If you think that it would be easy to hide these gifts, such a line of thinking proves the impropriety of accepting them.

Practical Exercises

Earlier in this book, you were asked to take it on faith that service-based leadership works, that your efforts to provide a meaningful, satisfying, challenging work environment for your employees would yield improved productivity and performance from your service team. The following exercises are meant to demonstrate that promise.

EXERCISE #1: Identifying Constituencies

Before you can effectively exercise your leadership skills, you must clearly recognize your various constituencies – those groups who depend on you and for whom you must provide leadership and service. For many positions this is fairly clear cut; there are customers, employees, and a boss. However, for some positions there may be other groups who rely upon your exercise of leadership.

In my current position on the corporate staff of a club management company, I also serve all operating departments in addition to the members and guests who ultimately pay our wages. To the extent I am successful in properly supporting and serving the operators, the more successful we as a company are in serving our members and clients.

So for every leadership position, one must identify the constituencies served. Once you have identified these, then make a list of each constituency's needs and how you and/or your team can best serve them. In most cases you need to visit with constituents to hear directly from them what they need or expect from you.

With a clear understanding of their needs, you are in a far better position to understand and execute your responsibilities and priorities.

EXERCISE #2: *Making Lists*

Ask your service team to make a list of the ten most frequent customer complaints and the ten most frequent customer requests. Give them several days to accomplish this. If they can't come up with ten, that's all right. The benefit in this exercise is not so much in the quantity of items, but in the overall process. Ask that they not compare their lists among themselves before giving them to you. They need not identify themselves on the lists unless they want to.

When you receive the lists, correlate and rank the complaints and requests. Share the results with your team in a meeting and ask for their input and help to address the complaints and meet the requests.

Some items will be relatively easy to deal with; others will be more complex and difficult. Involve your employees in designing solutions. Should any be too difficult or costly to resolve, share the reasons with your staff as appropriate. This exercise will accomplish several important things:

◆ It demonstrates to staff your desire and willingness to improve your operation.

◆ It shows your willingness to make your employees part of the decision process. To the extent you are able to listen to them and incorporate their ideas in the process, you will gain their trust and they will wholeheartedly support the solution.

◆ It will make your employees' jobs easier since they will be dealing will less customer complaints and more satisfied customers.

◆ It demonstrates to employees your commitment to customer service in that you care what your customers think and want.

Another variation on this theme would be to go back to your employees after you have resolved a good number of the items from their earlier lists and ask for two more lists – the most satisfying and the most frustrating things about their jobs. If you have established sufficient trust among your staff, this may open up further areas of improvement.

EXERCISE #3: Overcoming Obstacles

When I became general manager of my first hotel, I spent my initial weeks talking with the employees of various departments. In meeting with the housekeeping staff, I found a sullen group, who refused to make eye contact, barely responded to my comments, and asked no questions when given the chance.

I made a point over the next few weeks to visit housekeepers individually as they worked about the hotel. After several small-talk conversations with one particular housekeeper, I asked her how she liked her job. She proceeded to show me that her vacuum cleaner barely worked. This poor woman and every other housekeeper spent eight hours a day trying to clean carpets with vacuums that would not pick up trash and dirt. I couldn't imagine anything more defeating!

Within a week, we had new vacuums for the entire department. The cost was several thousand dollars – small change considering the impact it had on the cleanliness of the hotel and the morale of the housekeeping department. I also publicly praised the employee who made me aware of the problem. She became an overnight hero to her co-workers, and everyone understood by this positive reinforcement that management was serious about discovering problems and making improvements.

This story illustrates the next exercise.

Make it clear to your employees that you want to know what obstacles they face in the completion of their daily duties. Call a meeting of your team and ask them pointblank, "Is there anything I can do to make your jobs easier? Is there a better way to do this? What obstacles prevent you from doing your jobs efficiently? How can I help?"

Even if you don't get an initial response, establish and keep the lines of communication open. Keep probing with questions about their work, the challenges they face, and the obstacles that impede their efforts.

Sooner or later, they will open up. Hopefully, it will be a problem that will be totally within your power to solve. If it isn't, make every effort to convince your superiors of the necessity of change. Analyze the problem, explore alternative solutions, examine the cost/benefits of each alternative, do all your homework, and present your recommendation to your boss.

If your recommendation is accepted let your employees know and inform them of the timeline for implementation. If not accepted, find out why, explain it to your employees if appropriate, and be supportive of the decision. Continue to look for ways to eliminate obstacles. Revisit the decision periodically in an attempt to convince your boss of the necessity and value of the change.

Putting a positive emphasis on problem discovery and cheerfully following through to correct problems will demonstrate to all your employees your commitment to helping them and improving your operation.

EXERCISE #4: Expecting the Worst

At the beginning of my career, I would come in early to work on projects in the relative peace and quiet before the start of the business day. Once in a while I would arrive to significant problems.

The lobby was trashed from the night before, the early morning housekeeper called in sick, the morning banquet staff didn't have enough clean linen to set up, and so on.

Often these unexpected problems would ruin my day, and my anger and mood affected all around me. My reaction to events was making a bad situation worse.

In analyzing why this happened, I realized that my anger stemmed from disappointed expectations. I expected to come in early to accomplish things but was sidetracked by problems. Since I couldn't fully control the unexpected, I tried to focus on what I could control – my reaction.

The solution was to make a mental adjustment. Instead of coming to work expecting peace and quiet, I spent the time in my car thinking of all the things that may have gone wrong. When I arrived at work, one of two things happened:

- ◆ *If there were problems, I had anticipated them. The absence of disappointed expectations removed any sense of frustration and allowed me to focus on solving the problem.*
- ◆ *Most days everything was running smoothly which made me feel great. Instead of my bad mood ruining everyone else's day, my good feeling elevated all around me.*

This story illustrates an important point. As a supervisor you must take responsibility for yourself, your mood, and the profound impact you can have on your employees.

As an exercise, anytime you find yourself becoming angry with staff, stop, remove yourself physically from the situation, and analyze your anger. If you are honest with yourself, you will find that your anger has more to do with you than with your employees. Knowing that your anger stems from your disappointments, you must figure out ways to alter your expectations. None of your staff is perfect. Your team is made up of individuals with differing knowledge, skills, and abilities. Your role as a leader is to take advantage of their strengths while working on or accommodating their weaknesses.

Young leaders are often in a hurry to prove themselves. While your immediate accomplishments may prove impressive, in the long run it is the quality of your work relationships, the motivation and morale of your staff, and the depth of your team's organization and training that will demonstrate your worth.

EXERCISE #5: Getting Pumped Up

Everyone is subject to mood swings. Everything from biorhythms, to health, to the weather, to personal relationships, to the phase of the moon seems to affect a person's mood. While it is impossible to be "up" all the time, leaders cannot afford to be "down." It affects too many people who are depending upon them. But moods can be altered by conscious effort.

Professional athletes understand this important fact and routinely use it to ensure that they are "up" at the right time to achieve peak performance. The challenge in team play is to get most or all of the team pumped up for the big game.

Supervisors face the same challenge: how to get their team pumped up for the "big game," which in their case is everyday business. The first step, obviously, is to ensure that the leader is pumped up.

A simple exercise is to take a few moments before you leave home or in your car when you've arrived at work. Don't wait until you are at work, you may be overtaken by events and it will be too late. Take those few moments alone, close your eyes, and think about the tasks ahead of you that day, the desired outcome, and the enthusiasm necessary to carry you and your team through the effort.

Then put yourself through a cathartic routine to boost your adrenaline. This routine will be different for each individual, but to be effective, must physically engage your body in some fashion.

For example, you may chant, "Yes, yes, yes" with your eyes closed and fists clenched, or scream silently or out loud while pounding the dashboard, or beat on the seat while saying, "We can do it." Whatever works for you is OK, but you must feel your body consciously engage with your mind as you pump yourself up.

If this sounds crazy, think of the chest-thumping, helmet-bashing, head-butting routines used by professional football players to prepare for their games. While their "game" is more physical than customer service, your need to get "pumped up" for the game is just as real.

To further boost your mood, give the first person you meet an effusive greeting of good cheer. In the majority of cases that greeting will be echoed back to you. The positive reinforcement will lift you higher. Your resultant good mood and enthusiasm will fire up your staff and help them perform at the highest level.

While pumping up may seem silly to some, think of the alternative – a leader who comes to work in a bad mood which infects the entire staff. Instead of being fired up for the tasks at hand, they are moody, angry, and resentful – certainly in no frame of mind to offer quality service.

EXERCISE #6: Giving Thanks

This last exercise is simple and profound. Say thank you to your employees on a regular basis. Nothing could be simpler or more profound in its impact on staff morale because so few managers do it.

"Thanks for your help today," "I really appreciate your efforts on this project," "I realize how difficult this assignment was, and am most appreciative of your help," "I couldn't have done it without you," "You did a great job." – any of these expressions of appreciation, when sincerely given, will have a stunning impact on your service team.

Summary

Developing sound leadership skills is an evolutionary process. No one is perfect. Errors are made, but if you face them you will learn from your mistakes. The gradual accumulation over time of an understanding of what makes people tick, of what motivates and de-motivates, of what does and doesn't work, will eventually develop into a storehouse of common sense.

This accumulated wisdom should bring the leader to a state of profound humility. What gets accomplished is not so much a result of your efforts, but the efforts of your willing and committed employees. Your singular role is to articulate the vision and stand aside while coaching and cheerleading.

In reviewing a career, what often stands out are not your accomplishments, their luster having diminished with distance, rather it is the meaningful relationships you forged with employees, coworkers, customers, and bosses that will remain bright in your memory.

Thinking about this points directly and dramatically to where you should focus your attention, not inwardly on yourself and your ambitions, but outwardly on the quality of your interactions with others. This is the crux of service-based leadership.

RELATED ARTICLES

The following are articles by the author on a variety of leadership and management topics published over the years in various trade magazines. Each article reinforces or expands upon points discussed earlier in this work.

PERSONAL LEADERSHIP

Adding Value to your Organization

If you are interested in advancing your career, the easiest and quickest way to do so is to add value to your employer. When you consistently demonstrate your ability to take initiative, solve problems, and make your boss' job easier, you will be recognized as one who adds value to the organization. "Personal Leadership" will allow you to stand head and shoulders above your peers and will ultimately lead to greater and greater successes in life.

Reject the Status Quo

Every organization has its way of doing things. Often the methods are a result of stopgap measures implemented over time to deal with various problems as they arose. Seldom are standards, policies, and procedures formalized in writing; even less often are they well-thought out from a big picture standpoint. Despite the haphazard nature of most methods, they are considered sacred and untouchable by employees because "we've always done it that way."

A leader, however, does not accept this status quo. She shines the fresh light of reason on the organization, continually asking questions: Is there a better way to do this? Does this make sense? Does this really serve our customers' interests? This willingness to look for new ways to do things allows the leader to realize another principle.

Seek Constant Improvement

Every aspect of an operation – from product and services to standards, policies, procedures, work methods, and training material – should be analyzed for ways to do them better, faster, more efficiently, and with higher levels of service.

When a leader is dedicated to constant improvement and seeks the input of her employees, the entire department becomes energized with ideas, innovation, and enthusiasm. And while the organization as a whole and its customers benefit from the improvements, the employees gain the greatest benefit – knowing that their efforts contribute in a meaningful way to an organization that is vital and successful.

Be Proactive

A leader should always be looking ahead to ensure her department is ready for any contingency. Since most businesses have a seasonal routine, the leader reviews past activity from a variety of perspectives in a search for ways to improve performance, and she continually seeks new ideas, events, and activities to keep the operations interesting and fresh for customers.

Leaders should be looking at least three months ahead for routine operations, and further for major activities, events, or projects. This continually advancing planning horizon allows all essential requirements to be completed in a timely manner, while effectively implementing and marketing new products and services.

Have a Plan

Every event, activity, project, or initiative demands a plan. Without a proper plan a leader approaches everything helter-skelter, wastes valuable resources and time, and subjects employees to her own disorganization and lack of discipline.

By putting a plan in writing – even something as simple as a one-page outline of timing and responsibilities – a leader is better able to communicate with employees and with other affected departments. A written plan broadcasts a leader's competence and abilities to everyone who sees it.

The Army has a phrase to express the need for planning. The sanitized version of the six P's is:

"Prior Planning Prevents P. . .-Poor Performance"

Yet poor performance won't be prevented simply by planning.

Follow Through and Follow Up

Whatever she undertakes, the leader will follow through to ensure that all details are covered and all actions completed. Often follow through requires modification of the original plan when unexpected situations arise.

Lastly, the leader will follow up on all completed actions or projects to learn from mistakes and to ensure that the initiative met the expectations of customers, other managers, and employees.

Demonstrating Personal Leadership is more of a mindset than possessing specific skills. It involves the willingness to tackle any problem, the understanding that every problem has a solution, and the realization that problems are opportunities in disguise.

The choice to be a Personal Leader is up to you. You can tread water and wonder why your career isn't going anywhere; or you can add value to your organization and ensure your future success.

ORGANIZATIONAL LEADERSHIP

What does it mean to be an "organizational" leader? Much has been written to define what constitutes leadership, the role of the leader, and the habits of successful leaders. Though the exercise of all leadership is situational, the following traits can invariably be found in those who lead successful organizations.

Leading with a Vision

Moving large and complex organizations in a particular direction requires the ability to formulate and articulate a vision of what the organization should be. "Selling" the vision requires constant hammering home of easy-to-grasp themes. Without the "big picture" sense of direction, employees become lost in the day-to-day detail and monotony of their jobs. Leaders must engage with employees on all levels and view such interaction as an opportunity to "spread the gospel."

Transforming Vision into Day-to-day Action:

Long range vision must be broken down into a concrete plan of action for managers and supervisors at all levels. Annual plans, performance reviews, and goal setting sessions play an important part in establishing and communicating near and long term objectives. Many organizational failures result from faulty or inadequate communication of the vision. Informed employees are better employees. Leaders should strive to create an environment that facilitates communication flow where superiors and subordinates keep each other informed, quality and performance standards are communicated, feedback is constantly given, and every employee knows where the organization is going and how it will get there.

Having a Bias toward Action

Leaders accomplish something every day. There is an insistent time factor in management. New problems crop up continuously. When problems are not solved, the sheer volume of their accumulation can paralyze an organization. A leader's ideas, words, actions, and examples are major determinants in the success of any operation. No one should need to tell a leader what has to be improved in his organization. He should recognize what needs to be done, formulate a vision, and prepare an action plan to accomplish it.

Being Proactive in Finding Problems

Leaders do not have a negative attitude toward problems because they clearly signal where you should devote your time and energies. A famous inventor once said that he carried a notebook with him and noted each and every one of his daily irritations with the world around him. He understood if something irritated him, it most likely irritated everyone else. Finding a solution to the irritation often presented him with an idea for an invention or a business opportunity. The same principle applies to a leader who is on the lookout for problems. Invariably they point the way to some improvement in the operation. Further, when employees work for a leader who solves problems, they feel energized and empowered to do the same.

Knowing that Every Problem has a Solution

Every problem can be solved. It's merely a matter of priorities. Even the most complex problem can be broken down into its smaller solvable components. Sometimes a solution is the result of compromise or many little steps that contribute to an improvement in the overall situation. As much as possible, one should look for system solutions to problems, making their elimination part of the routine.

Paying Attention to Details

A good leader must have an eye for details. Much can be learned by observing an operation and a leader must spend a good deal of his time "out and about" to know what is going on in the organization.

Possessing High Standards of Quality

Leaders must establish and communicate their standards of quality. When employees are left to decide quality standards for themselves, the best that can be expected is inconsistent, and at worst, a complete absence, of quality and service.

Being a Strong Team Builder

Motivation and morale is built on making every employee part of the team. Organizational loyalty seemed to be the strong suit of Japanese corporations, but it is little more than a business version of the military's *esprit de corps*. Much of it goes back to pride and recognition, but it also depends upon building a strong organizational identity and constant communication. At the end of the day, without the willing and committed involvement of employees, the organization will never achieve its standards of excellence or high levels of success.

Having a Positive Attitude

Attitude is all-important in any endeavor. Employees look to leaders for guidance, reassurance, and example. A leader must learn to roll with the small ups and downs while keeping an eye on the larger vision. The proper attitude should also be mixed with an upbeat good cheer that is invariably infectious.

Instilling Dedication to Needs and Desires of Customers

The bottom line for any business is customer satisfaction. Shortsighted policies that have a negative impact on this satisfaction will eventually show up on the bottom line. The surest way to keep customers satisfied is to know what they want. Employees at all levels should be required to constantly seek the feedback and input of their patrons. Further, they should be instilled with a complete dedication to customer satisfaction.

Recognizing the Importance of Personal Selling

Perhaps the greatest marketing tool available is the committed involvement of leadership in selling. By becoming actively involved with customers and selling his product at every opportunity, the leader promotes not only the operation, but himself. Since many decisions are influenced by personal loyalties and first-hand recognition of competency, this type of salesmanship is often the most far-reaching and effective.

Effective and efficient operations in all areas of an organization are the direct result of good leadership. While sound management and technical skills are also important, without leadership the organization will never achieve its full potential.

FOCUSING ON SOLUTIONS

"Never complain – always occupy yourself with solutions."

This simple yet important maxim was brought home to me with stunning force years ago while working at a California resort. Here's the story:

Marjorie was the friendly head cashier at the resort and reported to the controller, who, as can be expected from someone in that profession, was a stickler for detail and accuracy. Among Marjorie's duties was the task of safeguarding the resort's large cash reserve bank and making change for the many cashiers. Her small office located in the administration building was frequently crowded with employees seeking change. Quite naturally, it was also a scene of noise and confusion.

One day on my walkabouts I stopped in to chat with Marjorie and was surprised to find her crying at her desk. When asked what was wrong, she responded tearfully that she was in danger of losing her job. Unaware that this was so, I asked why. She then related to me that, on multiple occasions during the past month, the resort bank came up short. Each time she was counseled by the controller, but at the last counseling her exasperated superior warned her that further shortages could result in termination. She went on to say that no matter how careful she tried to be, her bank was once again short. Through her tears she said she was sure she'd be fired this time.

As I sat across the desk from the distraught woman, I tried to calm her, but nothing I said could reassure her. Finally, in a sharp voice I said, "Marjorie, are you stealing from us?" Shocked, she looked at me incredulously and said quietly, "No! I could never do that." Having gotten her attention, I said, "OK, then, let's try to find out where the problem is." I then listened carefully as she described her daily routine for me.

Slowly, in response to my questions, she began to realize that counting errors were the natural consequence of the confusion of multiple employees engaging her in conversations while getting their change. Marjorie's native friendliness and outgoing personality were making it difficult for her to concentrate. I suggested that rather than going meekly to the controller to report yet another shortage, she should confidently go with a carefully thought out analysis of what was wrong and what steps she would take to overcome the problem.

As the two of us sat there reviewing the current procedures, Marjorie drew up a short list of how she could avoid future shortages.

1. *Replace the door to her office with a Dutch door that would remain closed and locked, thereby keeping employees out of her office.*

2. *Require employees seeking change to line up outside the door. This way she would deal with only one person and one transaction at a time.*

3. *Keep the large safe closed and locked while maintaining a smaller "par" change fund in a locked drawer at her desk. This way only a smaller amount of money had to be monitored and counted with each transaction.*

4. *Keep a log of all the change needs by each employee. Over time this record would allow her to establish the par fund at the appropriate level – neither too large nor too small.*

5. *Establish a policy that change for the largest cashier banks would only be made by appointment. This would allow her*

to be prepared for and deal with the largest transactions in a methodical way.

6. Establish set procedures for counting out change. Employees seeking change would use a change request form that itemized their needs. She also would establish a specific routine for multiple counts of tender and change while keeping tender separate from the par bank until all counts verified the transaction.

By the time I left her office, Marjorie had calmed down, galvanized by her plan to eliminate future problems. The next day she stopped me in the lobby to tell me that the controller was thrilled by her proposed "solutions" to an ongoing problem. He didn't want to fire her; he just wanted the problem solved.

Buoyed by the sense that she was now in control and that her job was no longer in jeopardy, Marjorie confessed that her preoccupation with the potential consequences of the shortages blinded her to a solution. She said it was a hard lesson learned, but one she would never forget.

It also made a great impression on me – one that I too still remember.

MANAGING YOUR BOSS

Five Easy Steps to Positive Perceptions

Just as a leader must manage available human, capital, and material resources to accomplish the mission, to be truly successful you must also manage the perceptions of superiors, in particular your immediate boss.

Why is this important? Shouldn't the boss be able to clearly recognize a subordinate's performance and progress? Not necessarily so. The boss:

- ◆ May work in another building, city, or state and may not have many first hand impressions.
- ◆ Is certainly busy with his own priorities.
- ◆ May have a number of other direct reports and can't focus sufficiently on any one.
- ◆ Is often focused on problems and underperforming areas, not on those operations that are running relatively smoothly.
- ◆ May be subject to the persuasive opinions of others who are not familiar with your performance or who may not have your best interests at heart.
- ◆ May have mistaken impressions based upon limited, partial, or biased perceptions.
- ◆ Can't be expected to be aware of all you are working on unless you tell him.

Ultimately, if the boss has a bad impression of you and your performance, you have no one to blame but yourself. So why leave it to chance? As a leader you must be as proactive about managing your boss as you are with other important areas of your life – family, finances, church or community, hobbies, and sports.

So how should you manage your boss' perceptions of your performance? The short answer is "information," but for practicality sake, here are five sure-fire ways to make a favorable impression.

1. Give your boss an honest, critical "State of the Union" report outlining the current realities of your operation. Never be afraid "to confront the brutal facts" as Jim Collins says in *Good to Great*, his groundbreaking book on successful companies. Support your analysis and the report with current operating benchmarks.

2. At the same time, present your "plan for improvement." I prefer to do this as an Annual Plan that will be updated each year as the state of the operation changes.

3. Provide brief monthly reports that update your boss on Annual Plan milestones and progress toward objectives.

4. Develop, track, and present your boss with meaningful benchmarks and analyses that demonstrate trends. Obviously, positive trends should be discussed, but negative ones also warrant discussion of planned corrective action.

5. When presenting or discussing problems in reports or in person, always present proposed solutions and plans of action at the same time. A boss, who continually receives a subordinate's problems without proposed solutions, may eventually realize he doesn't need the subordinate.

A few cautions are in order:

◆ Honestly identify and discuss problems. Overly optimistic
or continual rosy assessments invite skepticism and may
undermine your efforts. Remember that all operations have
problems and the first step in problem solution is problem
discovery.

◆ Don't over-promise and under-deliver. You must have a clear
grasp of what improvements your operation can realistically
make.

◆ When reporting operational successes, share the credit liber-
ally with your staff. When reporting or discussing failures,
reserve the blame for yourself. There is always more you
could have done!

Managing the boss is a skill like any other. Each boss may be a
little different in how he wants information presented and you should
take your cues from him.

Ultimately, a leader's job is to make a boss' job easier. To the
extent that you manage your operations successfully, make continual
improvements, and provide him with meaningful, timely, and useful
information, you will relieve the burden of his responsibilities while
making him look good. The usual outcome of doing this is to gain
your boss' trust and support for all that you do – and this is a great
start to a successful career!

DEVELOPING THE COMPETITIVE EDGE

Benchmarking Your Operations

Imagine two professional baseball teams. One team measures every aspect of every player's performance – the number of at bats; number of hits, walks, and strikeouts; batting averages against right- and left-handed pitchers; slugging averages; and fielding percentages. They also measure each pitcher's earned run average, number of base on balls, strikeouts, wild pitches, and so on. The other team decides it's too much trouble and keeps no statistics whatsoever.

These two teams will meet each other twenty times a season. While well-matched in player talent, hustle, and desire, and though each team possesses competent management and coaching, one team dominates the other season after season. Would anyone be surprised to discover which is the dominant team?

As everyone knows, this example is ludicrous because every baseball team measures player performance and uses this information to make crucial game decisions. What is it that baseball managers understand that some business managers don't seem to grasp? The fact that everything in life follows patterns. When patterns are tracked and analyzed, they can be used to predict future performance and assist the operation in a variety of other ways.

Benchmarking, the act of measuring and analyzing operating performance, seeks to understand the patterns underlying that performance.

Reasons to benchmark include:

◆ Establishing the baseline or 'benchmark' of existing operational performance.

◆ Comparing future performance to the benchmark.

◆ Establishing realistic performance goals for future periods.

◆ Comparing a particular period's performance with past periods, other similar operations, or an industry as a whole.

◆ Identifying under-performance or best practices.

◆ Improving the accuracy of budgets.

◆ Forecasting business levels.

◆ Measuring customer response to new products/services and initiatives.

◆ Providing hard numbers to support decisions and requests for additional resources.

◆ Establishing the condition of the operation when a new manager assumes charge.

◆ Establishing parameters for performance-based incentives.

A manager, like the pilot of a plane or the captain of a ship, needs to know that all systems are operating within desired parameters. How will he or she know without detailed measures of performance? While monthly operating statements provide good basic information, these summary numbers can mask troubling trends within the operation. For instance, higher food revenues can be a result of less patronage, but each customer spending more because of higher menu prices. The general manager is happy with the higher revenues, but is blissfully ignorant of declining customer patronage.

Benchmarking is best accomplished by managers with bottom-line responsibility. They have an absolute need to know and understand the underlying factors that affect their revenues and/or expenses. While different managers will need to decide what data is important to track, most performance measures will fall into the following broad categories:

- ◆ Revenues, both aggregate and by type
  - ○ Compare period to period.
  - ○ Track the underlying interplay of volume and average sale.
- ◆ Expenses
  - ○ Payroll is usually the single largest expense and bears the closest scrutiny.
  - ○ Other operating expenses, usually measured as a percentage of revenues.
- ◆ Inventories – Food, beverage, retail, and consumables.
- ◆ Retail sales mix to determine buying patterns of customers.
- ◆ Processes to track specific tasks or events.

Most of this raw data necessary to benchmark comes from point-of-sale (POS) reports. Much of the lode of daily information gets looked at briefly by managers or the accounting staff and is then filed away, rarely to be seen again. The real value of this information comes from tracking it over time to determine trends by day-of-week, week-to-week, month-to-month, and year-to-year. This makes it necessary for managers to pull the daily information from POS reports and enter it into standard, off-the-shelf spreadsheet software.

Even without sophisticated POS systems or computers, benchmarking can still be done. In the early days of my career I would spend the first half-hour of each day over coffee, manually tracking key data and benchmarks on graph paper. Now cash registers offer more easily-accessible data, and clearly, state-of-the-art POS systems provide the most information and flexibility of reports. Despite these reports, I still find it necessary to transfer daily data into electronic spreadsheets that allow me to archive data for future analysis.

A few caveats:

◆ There are as many aspects of an operation to measure as time, ingenuity, and resources will allow. Focus on those most critical to a department's operation.

◆ Data used in benchmarking must be defined and collected in a consistent manner.

◆ When comparing data, always compare like to like.

◆ Ensure benchmarks measure practices and processes with only one underlying variable. Multiple variables will still leave you in the dark as to the causes.

◆ Do not draw conclusions from too small a sample. The larger the sample the more accurate the conclusion.

◆ When two pieces of data are compared to generate a benchmark, either a small sample size or extreme volatility in one or the other, can skew the resultant benchmark.

Benchmarking is not complicated, but it does require organization and persistence. It is best accomplished by setting up routine systems to collect, compile, report, and analyze the information. Like a baseball team, the knowledge gained by benchmarking will bring an operation to the top of its game.

HAND IN GLOVE

Benchmarking and Budgeting

The first step in establishing an operating budget is to forecast revenues. Until some measure of anticipated income is projected, the level of variable payroll and operating expenses is pure guesswork. For existing operations, it is easy enough to look back at preceding years' revenues and project accordingly. It is far more difficult in startup operations where even the guesstimates of the most experienced operator are suspect.

Yet even with operating histories at hand, the person preparing the budget must have some understanding of the interplay of volume and average customer expenditure which underlie all revenue projections. This is important because the factors that bring a customer to an establishment are far different than those that influence how much he or she spends. These two measures – volume and average expenditure – are key items to benchmark in any operation and are easily determined from point of sale or cash register reports.

As an illustration I'll use a golf course operation, but the same would apply no matter what product or services are sold. In this simplified example, revenues come primarily from green fees, cart fees, merchandise sales, and practice range fees. The underlying volume benchmark is how many people use the golf course – the rounds of golf played.

By tracking these key revenues and golf rounds on a daily, monthly, year-to-date, and year-to-year basis, we can derive revenue per round benchmarks (shaded):

	Oct	Nov	Dec	Annual
Rounds of Golf	3,135	2,703	2,274	27,484
Revenues				
Green Fees	$66,875	$54,268	$44,569	$607,892
Cart Fees	$39,904	$33,267	$27,224	$352,852
Merchandise Sales	$5,295	$4,726	$6,790	$68,159
Practice Range Income	$4,148	$2,670	$3,323	$37,892
Revenue/Round Benchmarks				
Green Fees/Round	$21.33	$20.08	$19.60	$22.12
Cart Fees/Round	$12.73	$12.31	$11.97	$12.84
Merchandise Sales/Round	$1.69	$1.75	$2.99	$2.48
Practice Range Income/Round	$1.32	$0.99	$1.46	$1.38

Sample Benchmarks Computed by Dividing Revenues by Rounds

Recognizing that, absent significant change or abnormal events, the recent past is the best predictor of the future, these benchmarks can help project future rounds per period and revenues per round. All it takes is a little informed judgment and knowledge of upcoming events or trends that may impact the forecast.

By setting up a bank of data entry cells in a spreadsheet (shaded opposite), we define the assumptions underlying our revenue projections at the same time we create those projections. Nothing could be simpler – spreadsheet formulas are set up to automatically multiply the number of rounds by the benchmark for each revenue category to project future income.

Such clearly stated assumptions make it easy for superiors and owners who review the budget to understand how the projections were made. It also makes it easy for the operator who has missed his projections in a given period to go back and see why they were missed – either not enough customers (rounds of golf) or lower revenues per round.

Assumptions	Oct	Nov	Dec	Annual
Projected Rounds	3,300	2,800	2,250	28,550
Historical Benchmarks				
Green Fees/Round	21.40	20.15	18.75	22.20
Cart Fees/Round	12.75	12.35	12.00	12.90
Merchandise Sales/Round	1.75	1.85	3.05	2.50
Practice Range Income/Round	1.35	1.05	1.50	1.45
Projected Income				
Green Fees	$70,620	$56,420	$42,188	$633,810
Cart Fees	$42,075	$34,580	$27,000	$368,295
Merchandise Sales	$5,775	$5,180	$6,863	$71,375
Practice Range Income	$4,455	$2,940	$3,375	$41,398

Projected Revenues using Rounds and Revenue per Round Benchmarks

Once revenue projections are made, it is simple enough to forecast operating expenses if they have been benchmarked as a percentage of revenues. Therefore, if office supplies have historically run at 1.2% of revenues, then it's a good bet that, absent significant change, they'll continue to run at that level.

Given the magnitude of payroll costs in most operations, payroll can also be projected using volume (number of hours worked) and average hourly wage benchmarks. These are readily tracked since gross pay is a function of how many aggregate employee hours are worked and what the gross payroll amount is for any given pay period and, by extension, for the entire fiscal year.

My own experience with benchmarking for over 30 years has proven not only the practicality of benchmarking to better understand one's operation, but also the effectiveness of benchmarking as a tool for easy and accurate budgeting.

Make your work life easier by recognizing and utilizing the hand in glove relationship of benchmarking and budgeting.

THE ANNUAL PLAN

Would an NFL, college, high school, or for that matter, pee wee league football team play a game without weeks of practicing their plays and a game plan specifically geared to the team they're playing? Of course not! No matter how talented the quarterback and receivers, no matter how fast and hard hitting the linebackers, if the team doesn't know the plays, alignments, and game plan, their performance will be as chaotic and amateurish as a pick-up game in somebody's backyard.

Similarly, moving large, complex organizations toward a goal requires a leader with a plan. The leader starts with a vision of what the organization should be or accomplish. In ongoing operations the vision is usually of a qualitative nature. How well will the operation perform, what products and services will be offered, what level of service will be provided, what standards will be established. In some cases the vision will describe the accomplishment of specific projects or goals, such as a major renovation or a restaurant repositioning. Once defined, the leader must then communicate the vision and provide guidance to those who will translate the ideal into a reality. This guidance is the Annual Plan.

To be truly effective the plan must be written and shared. In its infancy the plan should be briefly and broadly sketched, but with each major goal stated clearly and succinctly. From the broad statement of goals, more detailed action steps and timelines can be developed. Responsibilities must be assigned and deadlines or milestones determined. When completed, the written plan must be shared with all responsible parties and, in most cases, with all employees to make them better informed and part of the team.

While such formal planning is normally associated with specific projects, during the latter stages of my hospitality career I prepared an Annual Plan each year prior to the budgeting cycle. My rationale was that as I defined for my subordinate managers what initiatives I intended for the coming year, each of them had to develop their departmental plan to coincide with the general plan. Often, their departmental plans affected their budget development. During budget review I could review the plans and any resultant impacts on overall revenues and expenses.

Just as it is important to do ongoing budget and operating reviews, it is also important to review progress toward completing departmental plans. Sometimes operating necessities require adjustments to plans or reallocation of resources. Despite delays and modifications, the process keeps any organization moving toward specific goals and the overall vision. Often, uncompleted plans and projects are rolled into subsequent year plans. Major benefits of such an Annual Plan are keeping staff focused on key elements of improvement and providing a more objective measure of managerial performance.

The following example for a start up private club shows how simple an Annual Plan can be.

CLUB ANNUAL PLAN

1. *Open club facilities/operations on schedule, in a professional manner, with high levels of member service.*

2. *Establish and maintain a robust schedule of member activities.*

3. *Meet or exceed the operating budget. Develop and submit next year's operating and capital budgets prior to November 1st.*

4. *Establish operating standards, policy, and procedure for all areas of club operation to include golf, tennis, activities, food & beverage, maintenance, housekeeping, security, accounting, and personnel.*

5. *Develop formal training programs for employees. Initial focus will be on the following positions:*
   ◆ *Golf operations staff*
   ◆ *Food & beverage staff*
   ◆ *Locker room/lounge staff*
   ◆ *Activities/pool staff*

6. *Establish a monthly club newsletter for members.*

7. *Assist in the design planning for the Activities Center and Clubhouse.*

8. *Develop a plan for a club network, allowing e-mail and database sharing among department heads.*

9. *Develop club web site and systems and procedures to communicate with members via e-mail.*

From this overall statement of goals, proceed to assign responsibilities for each task and establish a timeline for the accomplishment of each. The Activities Director, responding to the requirement of goal #2, might develop the following list of potential activities.

Possible Major Events

Member-Member Golf Tournament – early May
Member-Guest Golf Tournament – early October
Member-Guest & Member-Member Tennis Tournament
Easter Parade and Egg Hunt
Mother's Day
Father's Day
Memorial Day Celebration
July 4th Celebration

Labor Day Celebration

Oktoberfest

Harvest Festival

Halloween Party, Trick or Treating, Haunted House

Thanksgiving

Holiday Party

New Year's Eve Party (& alternative family celebration)

Possible Club Traditions

Lake Regatta - summer

Holiday Season Celebration (December Festival) – winter

Annual Lawn Party and Concert – spring

Oyster Roast – fall

Ongoing Activities

Golf Scrambles

Golf and Tennis Couples Night

Seniors Golf

Ladies Golf

Clinics, golf and tennis

Junior programs for golf and tennis

Swim Club

Specialty food nights

Happy Hour at the Cabana

Kids summer camps

Kids Club

Fitness training programs

Sightseeing trips

Once approved, she can begin to work with other key staff to set up an annual schedule of events.

The simple act of developing an Annual Plan establishes mutual expectations and galvanizes subordinate managers into action. In an ongoing operation where most of the standards, policies, systems, and traditions are in place, the plan is used to sharpen performance in specific areas of the operation, such as accounting, service training, golf cart cleaning and preventive maintenance, etc.

One helpful technique is to follow the example of the United Nations and dedicate each year to some aspect of operations, for instance, the Year of Formal Training, the Year of Innovative Activities, and the Year of Special Service Touches. Then each department head must devise a plan to create and implement initiatives for the designated focus in his area of the operation.

While an Annual Plan is both basic and simple to implement, many operations make no effort to prepare one. The unstated and unrealistic expectation is that each department head will show the initiative and teamwork to develop and implement a comprehensive and integrated plan of improvement and progress. Without leadership and an Annual Plan, the reality is a chaotic and amateurish operation, bush league in both conception and execution.

THE MISSION AND VISION STATEMENT

What We Do and How We Do It

Every business or organization provides a product or service for its customers and it's important that all leaders and employees understand the basic underlying premises of the company's function. This is particularly true in large, complex organizations where highly specialized managers and employees can easily become preoccupied with their own tasks and fail to recognize the imperatives of the larger effort.

This is why many companies, recognizing the danger of such a loss of focus, devise a mission and vision statement to concentrate their employees' efforts on the company's basic purpose. To be truly effective the mission and vision should be stated as simply and briefly as possible so that employees readily understand and remember their "reason for being."

What follows are a sample mission and vision statements with a brief italicized commentary for each. This particular company also added a list of guiding principles and operating standards to help its leaders and employees. This company is in the hospitality business, but many of the principles and characteristics apply to any business.

MISSION - *What We Do*

Understand and exceed the expectations of the customers and guests we serve.

Given that each customer or guest may have different expectations for the service we provide, it is up to all leaders to understand those expectations and then motivate their employees and organize their operations to exceed the expectations.

VISION - How We Expect to Do It

The Company is dedicated to enhancing the value of our customers' experience while distinguishing ourselves as a leading provider of hospitality services. We will do this through innovative products, programs, and services; customer-focused personalized service; and principled leadership.

Our customers expect value, service, and efficiency during every visit to our operations. We will exceed their expectations with innovative, industry-leading products, programs, and services. The service we provide will be fanatically focused on each and every customer, treating them as our ultimate employer. By doing these things we distinguish ourselves within our industry and ensure our success.

GUIDING PRINCIPLES -
Principles that Guide the Conduct of Our Business

The following principles define our performance and execution at all levels of the Company:

◆ Proactive leadership with a service-based philosophy.
Our leadership is active and engaged, while strictly adhering to service-based leadership principles.

◆ Forward-thinking, professional expertise.
Our professional knowledge should not only be up-to-date, but we should be constantly looking ahead for cutting edge concepts and business practices.

◆ Proven management and operating systems.

We utilize proven and well-documented management practices and operating systems to efficiently organize and operate our facilities.

◆ Sound planning and effective implementation.

All of our projects and tasks must be planned thoroughly and implemented completely.

◆ Innovative programs, continually reviewed.

We offer innovative products, programs, and services; and we continually review to improve them.

◆ Detailed benchmarks, constantly analyzed.

We benchmark all areas of our operations and analyze them for better performance and best practices.

◆ A commitment to staff development through formal, ongoing training.

We operate in a detail-intensive business and can only achieve excellence by thorough training and retraining.

OPERATING STANDARDS –
Standards that Form the Basis for Our Operations

The following standards form the foundation of our operations:

◆ Our vision and goals are articulated.

Our Strategic Plan lays out the long term goals for the Company. Each facility and operation prepares Annual Goals to serve as guides and targets for completion. We put these in writing to formally commit ourselves to their accomplishment.

◆ We are uncompromising in our commitment to excellence, quality, and service.

To serve our customers and operate at the highest echelons of our industry, we have established and are committed to the highest standards.

◆ Authority and responsibility are assigned and accountability assured.

Leaders are assigned both the authority and the responsibility to operate facilities or departments according to our standards. These individuals are held accountable for their results.

◆ We embrace innovation, initiative, and change while rejecting the status quo.

We seek constant improvement in all aspects of our operations.

◆ Standards are defined and operations are detailed in <u>written</u> policy and procedure.

Standards for our products, programs, and services are detailed in written policy and procedures so that nothing is left to chance.

◆ Customer problems are resolved politely and promptly to the customers' satisfaction.

No explanation needed.

◆ Constant communication and feedback enhance operations and service, while problems and complaints are viewed as opportunities to improve.

We can never communicate too much or too well. Informed employees are better employees. Problems brought to our attention allow us to focus on solutions.

◆ We benchmark revenues and sales mixes to evaluate customers' response to products, services, and programs, and we benchmark expenses, inventories, and processes to ensure efficiency and cost effectiveness.

We must pay close attention to what our customers are telling us by their spending habits. Benchmarking and analyzing expenses, inventories, and processes help us be more efficient and ensure our profitability.

◆ We ensure clean, safe, well-maintained facilities and equipment while safeguarding Company assets.

A good bottom line is only one measure of our effectiveness; we must also take care of our facilities and safeguard Company assets.

◆ We acknowledge each operation as a team of dedicated individuals working toward common goals and we recognize the ultimate value of people in everything we do.

While each employee has his or her own duties and responsibilities, every member of our Company works toward the common goal of understanding and exceeding the expectations of our customers and guests. Ultimately our business is about people and they must be valued and respected wherever and whenever encountered.

While mission and vision statements may seem obvious to those who have worked at the highest levels of an organization, they are essential for reinforcing the focus of mid-level and line supervisors, as well as being vital to the employees who interact daily with customers.

A DIFFERENT CAST OF CHARACTERS

While commiserating with a fellow hotel manager some years ago I said, "You know, Charlie, every hotel has the same set of problems, just a different cast of characters." Looking back from the vantage of a long career, I would now expand my original observation: every organization or business has the same set of problems caused or tolerated by a different group of familiar, but destructive characters.

Without strong and proactive leadership, the destructive potential of problem employees will be realized by co-workers and customers alike. And its not just the problem line employees who adversely affect the organization and the bottom line. "Problem" supervisors can be even more destructive.

My own early experiences as a line employee also support this view. I have worked for a few truly outstanding leaders, a great number of mediocre ones, and others that were just downright miserable. Examples abound!

◆ *I have a relative who works for a large governmental agency and the horror stories I hear from him are enough to make one cringe. Largely, the workplace seems to be filled with bosses and workers playing a vengeful game of rules and regulations. Much time is spent by all trying to discover loopholes and alternative interpretations of policy to get even with those who have crossed them. Lack of communication, purposefully keeping some in the dark while favoring others, constant calls to union reps to report supervisors, punishing errant employees with undesirable tasks or schedules are all part of the coping strategy. There are so many grievances and hearings; it's a wonder the organization gets anything done at all!*

◆ *A number of years ago a bright, young woman who worked for me had a chance to join a Fortune 100 company in what she described as her "dream job." In less than two years she was back with her own sad tales. Her bosses were unsupportive, seemingly more interested in their status and perks than in improving performance, and one boss' behavior was so aberrant she questioned his mental stability. As she said to me, "I'm sure I could have gone far and made big bucks if I had just stuck it out, but life is too short to devote time and energy to such madness." This same woman has risen far in our company and is just the kind of "A player" that any organization would be lucky to have.*

◆ *I once worked for a boss who was an alcoholic. Her inattention to her job and the tasks at hand was stunning, and it impacted all who worked for her. In reviewing our financial statements, it was clear that the business had been faltering for a number of years, yet the owners made no apparent moves to correct the situation or replace her. This realization led to my own early departure. I wasn't about to spend a portion of my life advancing an enterprise for which the owners seemed to care so little.*

◆ *A friend of mine teaches high school in a local public school district. The administration of her school is abysmal. Promotions and choice teaching assignments go to those favored by the principal instead of being based on merit or the best interests of the students. Not only is there no meaningful communication, but the principal is so out of touch with the faculty that he called a particular teacher by name over the intercom nearly three weeks after her tragic death in a car accident.*

Discipline at the school is spotty at best; rules for tardiness and dress codes are not uniformly enforced; kids roam the campus during class periods and shout obscenities at will; and no one seems to know what is going on.

At the end of every year teachers wonder what courses they will be teaching next year. Yet no one in the administration makes any effort to provide this critical information, allowing dedicated teachers to prepare or improve course material over their summer break. Finally, comprehensive test scores have fallen during each year of this principal's tenure.

Examples go on and on; there's:

◆ *The gossipy manager who has her favorite subordinates with whom she shares her contempt for other employees.*

◆ *The insecure department head who sees every competent subordinate as a threat to his position and treats them accordingly.*

◆ *The indiscreet owner of a small business who shares her most intimate personal problems with her office manager.*

◆ *The distant hotel general manager who rarely communicates with department heads. Lacking information, they fear the worst and trust no one. Naturally, there is little if any interdepartmental cooperation.*

These examples point to a deep and pervasive problem within organizations – the lack of competent leadership. The problem is so common it begs the question – where do we find leaders and why are they in such short supply? We know from hard experience that leaders don't spring by chance ready-made from the labor pool. While confidence, competence, and native ability play a big role, leadership, like any other skill, must be taught and learned.

First and foremost, though, owners and senior managers must recognize the need for effective leadership. All too often senior people seem so caught up in their own issues and agendas, they don't even recognize the necessity of sound leadership throughout their organizations. Secondly, they must possess the willingness to develop leadership skills among first-time and junior supervisors – they must possess the will to make it happen. Some, realizing their short tenure at the top, may be unwilling to devote precious time and energy to an endeavor that may take years to show results. Regardless of the reasons, without proper training and the inspiring example of leaders above them, young managers, with rare exceptions, will not develop the necessary skills and abilities to become strong leaders.

And without strong leadership, any organization will have the same, common set of problems, and will limp along, differentiated only by its own uniquely familiar cast of characters.

EXERCISING LEADERSHIP

Respect, Not Like!

One of the basic tenets of leadership is that being a leader is not a popularity contest. Leaders need to make tough, often unpopular, decisions and can't be swayed by group opinions. It is often said that followers don't have to like their leaders; they just have to respect them.

There is truth in these maxims which are wonderfully dramatized in the classic World War II movie, *Twelve O'Clock High,* a film widely used to teach leadership principles. Gregory Peck, in the starring role, plays General Frank Savage, an Army Air Corps officer sent to take temporary command of an underperforming and demoralized bomber squadron.

In a telling scene that clearly demonstrates the "role playing" element of leadership, Savage wants a last, quiet moment before putting on the mantle of demanding leadership to whip the squadron into shape. Riding in his staff car just outside the gate of the air base he tells his driver to pull over. The two get out and Savage offers the young enlisted man a cigarette. It's clear in that brief moment that the General feels kindly toward his driver and treats him accordingly.

The moment over, he crushes the cigarette under his heel, adjusts his cap, and climbs back into the car. Seconds later at the gate, the sedan comes to a screeching halt; Savage gets out, and chews out the enlisted guard for his laxity on duty. Clearly, the General has arrived with a mission.

As he takes on the demoralized and battle-weary flight crews, his tough, single-minded approach creates a backlash of resentment, leading all the crews to put in for transfers out of the unit. The unit's adjutant, a peacetime lawyer played by Dean Jagger, realizes that the new commander is trying to shake the men out of their self-pity and stalls for time – just enough time for Savage to begin rebuilding the men's pride and fighting spirit.

Another movie that touches on the same themes is *Hoosiers*, in which Gene Hackman plays a disgraced college basketball coach, Norman Dale, who comes to small town Indiana to coach a high school basketball team. His focus on the fundamentals of the game, unorthodox style, and early season losses turn the town against him, but he and his team ultimately prevail by winning the state championship, becoming the smallest school ever to win the title.

While both Frank Savage and Norman Dale found themselves in situations where they followed leaders who were popular with their subordinates, these two lead characters understood it was more important to achieve results than to be popular or liked. In time their disgruntled followers came to understand and respect them – precisely because their leadership led to success.

The simple lesson is that what most employees really like has more to do with sound leadership than popularity. Consider that most people:

- ◆ Like to do a good job and take pride in their work.
- ◆ Like to know that what they do contributes.
- ◆ Like to receive feedback on their efforts.
- ◆ Like to know the major decisions that affect their organization, their work, and their jobs.
- ◆ Like a fair and consistent boss, one who demands excellence of himself and others.
- ◆ Like to understand the big picture.

♦ Like to be treated with dignity and respect.

♦ Like to work for a competent and dynamic boss.

♦ Like to be properly trained to do their job.

♦ Like to have an interest taken in them as individuals.

♦ Like to work for a successful and efficiently operated enterprise.

So workers may not like their boss in the sense of being a buddy, but they certainly like a boss who, by the exercise of strong leadership, improves their work life, recognizes their efforts, and makes their enterprise successful.

Do the rights things as a leader and your followers will respect and admire you – which, in the final analysis, is far more important and satisfying than having them like you!

BUILDING A DISCIPLINED ORGANIZATION

A leader desires excellence and success in her business, and she understands that these goals are dependent upon the quality and commitment of staff. It must also be clear that discipline is necessary to maintain the direction and focus of any organization and to establish and maintain standards of quality and service.

Unfortunately, in every group of employees, there are some who will develop attitude problems, lack commitment, or become incapable of meeting established standards. When confronted with such a problem employee, it is the responsibility of the leader to deal quickly and effectively with the situation before it degrades the efforts of the rest of the staff.

Leader's Responsibility

It does no good to have standards, policies, and procedures spelled out, if they are not going to be enforced. Whenever a leader overlooks an infraction, she encourages others to similar violations. A lax leader can be more damaging than no leader at all.

Further, a leader is expected to actively confront any problem employee in her department with the aim of correcting the problem. If it cannot be corrected in a reasonable period of time, the leader is expected to terminate the individual while following appropriate termination policies.

Disciplinary Philosophy

A successful leader will subscribe to the "hot stove" approach to discipline. She tells employees what is expected of them and what the consequences are of ignoring standards, policies, and procedure. If they then touch the hot stove, they get burned.

The rationale behind this philosophy is that she wants to deal with staff as adults who are responsible for their own actions, and she wants to avoid inconsistency.

Good Communication

Good communication is important when working with a troubled or problem employee. Some leaders do not like to confront staff on seemingly "small" issues. As a result, many small problems build up until the leader finally blows her top and is ready to fire the employee. However, termination is inappropriate because the leader has not previously discussed the problems with the employee, warned him of the consequences of continued problems, or offered any help to correct the problem.

Good communication will prevent this situation. If the leader talks frequently with employees, points out minor problems as they occur, and addresses continuing problems in a proactive and formal way, an employee will not be caught by surprise should he be terminated.

Consistent Communication

Her philosophy requires that she consistently tell staff what she expects of them. First, she does this by spelling out in detail her requirements by creating an employee handbook. Second, she expends some effort through orientation and formal training to make staff fully aware of their responsibilities and her expectations.

Fairness and Consistency

A leader's disciplinary process must be fair and consistent. This will follow naturally from standards, requirements, policies, and procedures being applied fairly and consistently to all employees. Leaders who are not fair and consistent will create major problems within their organizations. There is no quicker way to destroy morale and trust than to play favorites.

Often the perception of fairness is as important as the reality. Leaders should not only be fair, but also give all appearances of being fair. If some special situation comes up where a decision may seem unfair to some employees, the leader should take the time to explain the situation to everyone. This will "clear the air" and more than likely satisfy staff.

Constructive and Progressive

A disciplinary process should be designed to be both constructive and progressive. By this it is meant that all disciplinary actions are aimed at correcting erroneous or inappropriate behavior, and successive disciplinary actions will be progressively more severe. These two aspects are, in reality, part of the same philosophy. While a leader wants to help employees overcome their problems, when the problems continue, she wants to get the employee's attention with progressively more severe consequences.

Higher Standards for Supervisors

Because of the position, experience, training, education, and other factors that led to hiring, leaders are held to a higher standard of conduct and performance than line staff. In disputes between staff and leaders, it is expected that the superior will have solidly documented cases showing thorough investigation of any incident.

While leaders will always be supported when in the right, line employees should be given the benefit of the doubt when there is insufficient evidence or the absence of a thorough investigation. The best way for a leader to ensure that she is supported in her decisions is to have all facts together before taking disciplinary action.

Summary

Establishing and maintaining discipline in an organization is one of the core responsibilities of a leader. But it must be done in a reasonable, fair, and consistent way that contributes to good morale and improved performance, as well as in a way that protects the leader and the company from wrongful termination and discrimination lawsuits.

Reasonable, fair, and consistent discipline is inherently easy if a leader sincerely values her employees, tells them what is expected, and then holds them to a standard as adults responsible for their own moods and actions. While this may be a challenge for some employees, the majority will willingly accept a disciplined organization when they know that everyone, including the leader, is held to the same high standards.

FREEDOM TO FAIL

As an Army Captain, Pete Dawkins (West Point class of 1959, Heisman Trophy winner, First Captain of the Corps of Cadets, in the top of his class in academics, followed by a distinguished military and business career) wrote a seminal article entitled "Freedom to Fail" which was published in Infantry Magazine.

In this article Dawkins said that the Army's Officer Efficiency Report (OER) system that demands perfection of officers who wished to advance their careers, risked damaging the effectiveness of the officer corps. Any officer who did not repeatedly have the highest score on his OER could not expect choice assignments or rapid promotion. "All too often," he said, "the basis on which (officers) are compared is the absence of 'blemishes.' The ideal almost seems to be the man who has done so little – who has exerted such a paltry amount of initiative and imagination – that he has never done anything wrong."

As Dawkins aptly points out, failure can be the greatest teacher we have. It fosters critical review of the actions leading to the failure, while success breeds complacency and acceptance of the status quo.

Another military example: in July 1863, Confederate General James Longstreet watched three divisions under his command severely repulsed in the disastrous Pickett's Charge at Gettysburg. Longstreet had been opposed to Lee's plan for a multi-division assault on a broad front, but was overruled by his superior.

Several months later, Longstreet used the lesson learned from that defeat to launch a successful attack against Union lines at Chickamauga. This time he formed his attacking force into columns of divisions to deal a sharp and irresistible blow that shattered the Union line and routed nearly a third of Rosecran's Army of the Cumberland.

So what does this lesson from military history have to do with business management? Plenty! Leadership is leadership no matter what the enterprise or situation. Any leader who creates an organization where leaders are not given the freedom to fail, risks the larger failure of mediocrity.

Leaders should give their subordinates plenty of latitude to figure out how to solve problems or plan projects without being micro-managed by their bosses. Subordinates should be encouraged to formulate and execute bold and innovative ideas. Certainly failure will occur, but rather than blaming those responsible, encourage subordinates to conduct rigorous in-depth reviews of what went wrong and how things might have been done differently. The critical review process is the opportunity to learn and grow. Serious and sincere soul-searching for answers will inevitably lead to understandings that will improve future performance.

Having extolled the upside of mistakes let me also add that some errors are so egregious and obviously foolish that they call into question the subordinate's judgment. While no leader can ensure that all his subordinates have basic common sense and good judgment, he can monitor their work to avoid the worst mistakes.

Such monitoring is made much easier when there is good, open communication between the leader and subordinates. Conversely, an uncommunicative leader helps create the environment where subordinates acting on their own are afraid to approach the leader to seek advice and guidance. In this situation the failure is the leader's.

Things every leader/manager should do to encourage initiative:

◆ Do not micro-manage. Give subordinates broad directions and desired outcomes, but allow them to formulate and execute the details.

◆ Foster good two-way communications so that subordinates keep you informed of progress and are unafraid to seek advice.

◆ When giving guidance, explain the why's as well as the how's so that subordinates gain a broader understanding of your thought processes.

◆ When mistakes are inevitably made, do not get angry. Instead, be supportive and require subordinates to conduct a *post mortem* to determine what went wrong and what might have been done differently.

◆ Don't be afraid to give the failing subordinate new opportunities to prove his or her abilities. In other words, when he gets thrown from his horse, make sure he gets back up on it again.

Failing is an inherent and useful part of human growth. Make sure your subordinates have the "freedom to fail."

GETTING THE RIGHT PEOPLE ON THE BUS

Good to Great, a book by Jim Collins, describes the ground-breaking study of run-of-the-mill publicly-traded businesses that transformed themselves into great companies, each significantly outperforming the general stock market for fifteen or more years. Jim and his research team at Stanford University School of Business wanted to know what these companies did that made them so spectacularly successful. His findings are surprising, in some cases at odds with the common wisdom, and are based upon empirical evidence, not management or business theory.

One of the findings is that the good-to-great companies began their transformation by hiring the right people, or as he puts it, "getting the right people on the bus," and conversely, "getting the wrong people off the bus." While this concept of finding and hiring the right people seems commonsensical, it is surprising that out of 1,435 companies initially screened for the study, only 11 made the cut as good-to-great organizations – and all eleven sought first to hire the right people before they decided what they must do to transform themselves.

For those of us struggling with the daily challenges of our operations, the question arises, "How do we know we are getting the right person on the bus?"

While there are many different approaches and techniques for trying to find the right person for a position, the Disney Corporation has developed a successful hiring model that weeds out applicants who do not demonstrate the "right stuff" for Disney. They do this with the clear understanding that they only want to hire the bright, energetic, positive, outgoing people that make any visit to Disneyland or Disney World such a pleasant experience.

The CEO of a large hospitality and service company wanted to establish a similar model that presented a series of screenings to cull the applicant pool to a smaller group who possessed certain traits. The model devised worked like this:

1. Applications are taken at the Human Resource Office (HRO) by appointment only or only during designated hours.

First screening	*Can applicants follow direction? Are they interested enough in working for us to make an appointment?*

2. At the appointment, before they are given an application to fill out, they are asked to read the "Company Requirements and Standards" – a printed sheet explaining the company's high standards and giving an overview of the corporate culture, dress and grooming standards, and accountability for standards and performance.

Second screening	*Are applicants on time for the appointment? Are they professionally or appropriately dressed and groomed? Are they scared off by the standards and requirements? What is their attitude and demeanor while interacting with the HRO staff?*

3. Applications are reviewed for information provided and qualifications.

Third screening	*Is the application complete and legible? Does an applicant have the right qualifications for the position? Do they provide current contact information for references?*

4. Applications of qualified persons who pass the first three screenings are sent to the hiring manager for interview consideration. Managers conduct initial telephone interviews and then hold mandatory face to face interviews. At that interview applicants are given a copy of the detailed dress and grooming standards for the position.

Fourth screening	*How is their telephone presence? Do they walk into the interview with purpose and introduce themselves with a handshake and a smile? Are they enthusiastic and positive in describing their experience and what they can bring to the company? Do they have any hesitation or issues with the dress and grooming standards?*

5. Once hired, new employees are scheduled for a New Employee Orientation (NEO) before they begin working. If the new employee do not come to the NEO on time or in appropriate dress (without compelling reason), they are terminated.

Fifth screening	*Are they dependable and do they understand the appropriate professional dress?*

Applicants are treated in a perfunctory manner (professional, no-nonsense, somewhat aloof) until they are brought into the fold. Then the "selling" of the company and rah-rah excitement begins.

While all of this seems like a lot of effort to hire a server, housekeeper, or cart attendant, consider the consequences of hiring a person with an attitude problem, who has issues with the company culture or policies, or one who doesn't have the character and personality traits to be a successful service employee. At best, the manager will have to hire all over again, possibly after investing considerable time and energy in training; at worst, repeated poor service situations could damage the business.

The real work in a screening process is the initial organization and set up. Once up and running, the process may actually save the organization significant man-hours in interviewing, hiring, processing, training, and terminating the wrong people that were allowed on the bus.

In *Good to Great* Jim Collins finishes the chapter on hiring the right people with the following observation:

> **"The old adage**
> **'People are your most important asset' is wrong.**
> **People are not your most important asset.**
> **The <u>right</u> people are."**

THE ULTIMATE VALUE OF PEOPLE

◆ Without employees there would be no successful business leaders.

◆ Without customers there would be no money to pay employees.

◆ Without owners willing to risk their capital there would be no businesses to hire employees.

The distinguishing characteristic of these three statements is that they all involve people. And while every person is an individual, unique in background, experience, and education, the great majority have a common set of needs as they negotiate their worlds. They:

◆ Wish to be treated well, with dignity and respect.

◆ Want value for their labor given or money spent; in other words, they don't want to feel cheated.

◆ Want to know what's going on and appreciate timely and accurate information that affects them.

◆ Prefer to trust and be trusted.

◆ Appreciate kindness and generosity of spirit, especially when unexpected.

◆ Recognize someone who is principled and whose words and actions are grounded in values.

◆ Want to be recognized for who they are, not lumped into some great unknown, and often unnoticed, mass.

While any person can hold a position of authority, true leadership and its attendant success flows naturally from that person who recognizes the ultimate value of people in all he or she does.

While this seems trite, my experience has clearly confirmed that the majority of managers and supervisors do not intuitively understand this critical point. Many are so wrapped up in their own ambitions and agendas they seem oblivious to those around them. And this is a recipe for personal and professional failure as demonstrated by the following story.

Several years back I was at the checkout counter of the local outlet of a national home improvement chain. As I placed my purchases on the counter to be scanned, the cashier began complaining about the lack of adequate cashiers on duty and then rambled on, expressing a general dissatisfaction with her bosses and the company. Not anxious to know all her issues with her employer, I was noncommittal in my responses; yet on and on she went. I couldn't wait to get away.

While I was in the midst of a major do-it-yourself home renovation and making frequent trips for supplies and materials, I began driving an extra mile or two to a competitor store where the selection and pricing was comparable, but the staff seemed more contented and committed to service.

Having discovered the new, happier store, I spent and continue to spend a considerable sum of money with them. The disgruntled employee may have been an isolated case, yet service-based leaders should have been available for her concerns or, by being more closely engaged with the staff, discovered her "attitude" problem and resolved it without losing a potentially good customer.

In today's busy world where convenience, location, pricing, and technology drive many purchase decisions, the human touch is often overlooked. Yet I know half a dozen employees at my favorite home improvement store by name and have periodically written letters of commendation to their company when they are particularly helpful. This is the way I prefer to do business. While I may not be in the majority, I can't help but believe there are many others like me who enjoy friendly human contact. When major corporations are vigorously contending for a few percentage points of market share, the human touch inherent in service-based leadership should not be overlooked. People matter! And true leaders understand this.

About the Author

Ed Rehkopf is a graduate of the U.S. Military Academy and he received a Masters of Professional Study degree in Hospitality Management from Cornell's School of Hotel Administration. During his long and varied career, he has managed two historic, university-owned hotels, worked at a four-star desert resort, directed operations for a regional luxury-budget hotel chain, opened two golf and country clubs, and currently manages projects and directs communication and training for East West Partners Club Management.